Crete

COLLINS
Glasgow & London

First published 1990

Printed and Published by
William Collins Sons & Company Limited
ISBN 0 00 435776-0

HOW TO USE THIS BOOK

Your Collins Traveller Guide will help you find your way around your chosen destination quickly and easily. It is colour-coded for easy reference:

The blue-coded 'topic' section answers the question 'I would like to see or do something; where do I go and what do I see when I get there?' A simple, clear layout provides an alphabetical list of activities and events, offers you a selection of each, tells you how to get there, what it will cost, when it is open and what to expect. Each topic in the list has its own simplified map, showing the position of each item and the nearest landmark or transport access, for instant orientation. Whether your interest is Architecture or Sport you can find all the information you need quickly and simply. Where major resorts within an area require in-depth treatment, they follow the main topics section in alphabetical order.

The red-coded section is a lively and informative gazetteer. In one alphabetical list you can find essential facts about the main places and cultural items - 'What is La Bastille?', 'Who was Michelangelo?' - as well as practical and invaluable travel information. It covers everything you need to know to help you enjoy yourself and get the most out of your time away, from Accommodation through Babysitters, Car Hire, Food, Health, Money, Newspapers, Taxis and Telephones to Zoos.

Cross-references: Type in small capitals - **CHURCHES** - tells you that more information on an item is available within the topic on churches. A-Z in bold - **A-Z** - tells you that more information is available on an item within the gazetteer. Simply look under the appropriate heading. A name in bold - **Holy Cathedral** - also tells you that more information on an item is available in the gazetteer under that particular heading.

Packed full of information and easy to use - you'll always know where you are with your Collins Traveller Guide!

Photographs by ***Phil Springthorpe***

INTRODUCTION

The island of Crete is a continent in miniature. In the course of one day you can cross a breathtaking mountain range, wander through an orange grove in the throbbing heat of a coastal plain, and slide thankfully into a clear, blue-green sea at a shady beach. It is an island rich in scenic contrasts and redolent with the history of 5000 years.

Crete is the largest and most southern of the Greek islands and the fourth-largest island in the Mediterranean, lying almost equidistant from mainland Greece and the Turkish and North African coasts. Its long, thin shape provides about 650 miles of coastline, and its long, blazing summers ensure its popularity as a major tourist centre.

When you arrive on Crete, whether by sea or air, the first thing that strikes you is the ruggedness of the treeless terrain. In almost every direction you look there are massive, brooding mountains shimmering in the haze. The spectacular White Mountains (Lefka Ori) lie to the west. Mount Ida (Psiloritis), often snow-capped as late as May, dominates the central range and the Dikti Mountains, with the famous cave said to be the birthplace of Zeus, King of the Olympian gods, is further east. Lying on a hot beach within reach of the cooling sea, you might feel it too great an effort to struggle up into the mountains, but the effort once made is well repaid - the views are awesome and ever-changing, the breezes cool, and rock and sky fuse in the brilliant light. The mountain roads swoop round bends into tiny olive groves, past villages of white-washed houses which cling to the mountainside. Although Crete is largely mountainous, the coastal and upland plains are often unexpectedly green and lush with intensive crops of tomatoes and melons.

The island has many beaches to please sun-loving people, from wide sweeps of dark golden sand to secluded rocky coves. If you have transport, or are prepared to walk, it is still possible, particularly on the south coast, to find undeveloped beaches with few visitors.

Crete has had a long and turbulent history and, it must be remembered, has only been part of Greece since 1913. Before then the island was in the hands of the Turks for two-and-a-half centuries, and before that there were four centuries of Venetian rule. In fact, ever since the decline of the great Minoan civilization, possession of Crete has been fiercely contested. The island was taken by Rome in 67 BC, by Byzantium in AD 395, by the Arabs in AD 824, retaken by Byzantium in

AD 961, and sold to the Venetians in 1204 for 1000 silver marks. But Cretans have always resisted invaders fiercely. Throughout the centuries they have risen in rebellion against their various overlords, as was also demonstrated in the Second World War during the German invasion of the island, when many Cretans took to the mountains and, along with their allies, waged guerilla warfare to regain their freedom. Out of this rich and diverse past the Minoan civilization stands supreme. Flourishing from about 2500-1400 BC, the Minoans created a

distinctive culture that is regarded as Europe's first great civilization. Their palaces and frescoes, their pottery and jewellery were unrivalled in the ancient world, and the kingdom of Minos, with its extensive trade links, held sway over most of the Aegean. But the dividing line between history and legend is often hazy. Was Minos one king or the name of many kings? What exactly was the dreaded Minotaur, said to be half-man, half-beast (the result of an unnatural lust for a bull wished on Minos' wife by a vindictive god)? One of the frescoes in Heraklion's Archeological Museum shows a slim bull-leaper vaulting gracefully over the horns of a bull. Was this a sport, or a ritual performed by the young sacrificial victims before being devoured by the Minotaur?
There is so much to see on Crete: archeological sites from Minoan and later periods, Byzantine monasteries and churches with their beautiful icons, Venetian fortresses, huge and impressive caves, spectacular mountain gorges - it would take a year to see and appreciate it all. But above all, the visitor should try to visit the two great Minoan palaces at Knossos and Phaestos. Go first to the world-renowned Archeological Museum in Heraklion and view the wonderful Minoan artefacts from the sites before going to Knossos itself, just five km away, to see the partly-reconstructed palace. Visiting the Palace of Phaestos, in the south of the island, will take up a whole day, leaving from Heraklion, but the beauty of its setting is unsurpassed.
Crete has something for everyone. With the increase in tourist developments many of the towns and resorts have acquired quite a cosmopolitan air, with continental-style restaurants, souvenir and craft shops, and fashionable bars and discos. But still the contrasts persist. Behind the hurly-burly of Rethymnon and Chania's lively seafronts there are the charming, narrow streets of the old Venetian quarters, where minarets and shells of Venetian *palazzi* bear witness to Crete's turbulent past. If your preference is for a sun-and-sea holiday, there are many busy resorts offering all kinds of entertainment, from water sports and boat trips, to inland coach tours. For the energetic, there is the 18-km trek through the spectacular Gorge of Samaria and walks in the mountains or along the dramatic south-west coast, where the mountains seem to plunge straight into the sea. But take care and go well-prepared - Crete is a rugged place.

Tourism has inevitably left its mark on this most Greek of Greek islands and its proud and hospitable people.The north coast, in particular, is quite heavily developed in many places, and some formerly quiet fishing villages in the south now throng with summer visitors. But ancient traditions die hard, and Crete is a big island. Off the beaten track, in the less frequented coastal and mountain villages, the visitor's few words of Greek - *kalimera* (good morning) or *efkaristo* (thank you) - will be greeted with welcoming smiles and hospitality. If you can, it is worth hiring a car for a few days to cross one of the mountain ranges, perhaps taking in a monastery or Minoan site on the way, and heading for one of the more remote villages on the south coast, where you can sit in a taverna by the beach with a glass or two of *retsina* or a cool beer, a plate of grilled red mullet and a Greek salad, and watch the sun sinking lazily into the Aegean Sea.

Days on Crete pass very pleasantly, and however you spend your time on the island - swimming, sunning, exploring mountains, caves, monasteries or Minoan ruins - you will not easily forget what Homer called this 'land of Crete in the midst of the wine-dark sea'.

Jennifer Bassett

HERAKLION
Archanes
Kastelli
Malia
Neapolis
Elounda
Elounda Beach
GULF OF MIRABELLO
Agios Nikolaos Beaches
Agios Nikolaos
Amoudhara Beach
Istro Beaches
Males
Ano Viannos
Ierapetra
Ierapetra Beaches
Ferma Beach
Mirtos Beach
Agii Deka
Sitia
Sitia Beach
Vai
Vai Beach
Zakros

AGIOS NIKOLAOS

Four busy beaches near town accessible by bus or on foot.
Ammos and the municipal beach - both small and shingly. Sandy beaches at Ammoudi, ten minutes to the north, and Almiros, two km to the south.

ELOUNDA

11 km north of Agios Nikolaos. Regular bus service.
Shallow, pebble bays with clear water ideal for snorkelling. Submerged city.

AMOUDHARA

5 km south of Agios Nikolaos. KTEL Sitia/Ierapetra bus.
Clean, quiet, sandy beach easily reached from the road. Tavernas nearby.

ISTRO

9 km south of Agios Nikolaos near Kalo Horio. KTEL bus.
Small, pleasant, sandy beaches a few minutes from the road.

SITIA

70 km east of Agios Nikolaos. KTEL Sitia bus.
Long, busy, sandy beach. A bit dirty, but with cafés nearby. *See* **EXCURSION 1**.

VAI

23 km north east of Sitia. Bus from Sitia daily.
Exotic sandy stretch with palm trees and green waters. Busy. *See* **EXCURSION 1**.

IERAPETRA

36 km south of Agios Nikolaos. Regular bus service.
Long, sandy beach by this sizeable south-coast resort. *See* **EXCURSION 1**, **A-Z**.

FERMA

10 km east of Ierapetra.
Idyllic little bay with clear, clean, shallow water.

MIRTOS

15 km west of Ierapetra. Bus from Ierapetra.
Long, clean beach of dark sand and shingle beside an attractive village.

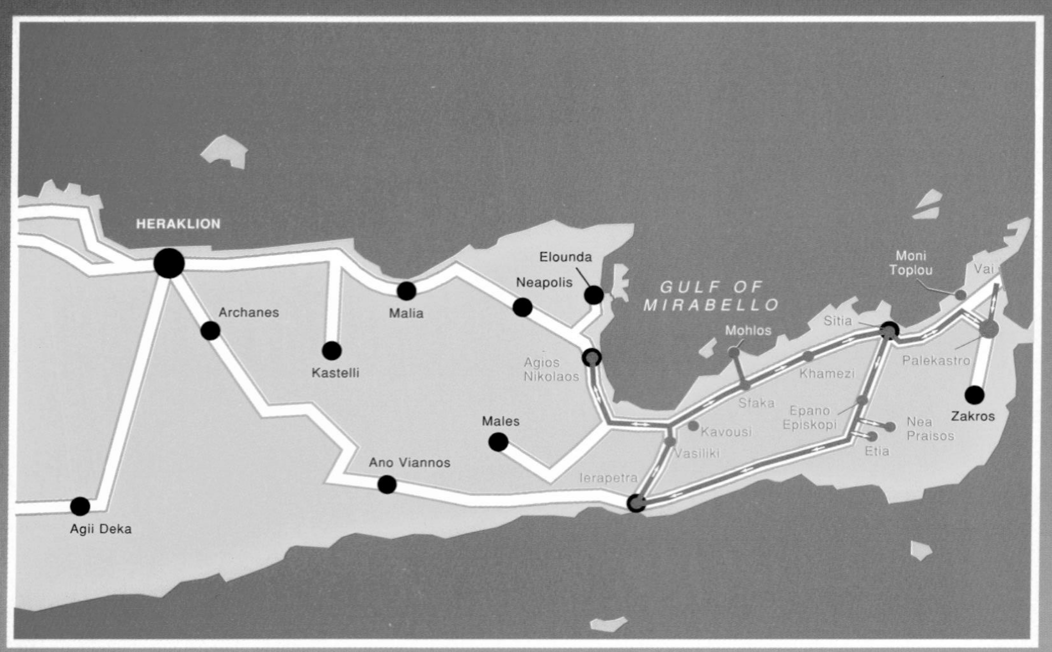
HERAKLION
Archanes
Agii Deka
Kastelli
Malia
Ano Viannos
Neapolis
Elounda
Males
Agios Nikolaos
GULF OF MIRABELLO
Ierapetra
Vasiliki
Kavousi
Mohlos
Sfaka
Khamezi
Epano Episkopi
Sitia
Moni Toplou
Vai
Palekastro
Nea Praisos
Etia
Zakros

Excursion 1

272 km. *Two-day excursion to Sitia, Moni Toplou, Palekastro, Vai, Episkopi, Nea Praisos, Ierapetra and Vasiliki, stopping overnight at either Sitia, the largest town in the area, or the smaller resort of Palekastro (you will be passing through both places twice).*

Take the main road out of Agios Nikolaos towards Sitia and begin to enjoy some of the fine views over the Gulf of Mirabello.
26 km - **Kavousi**. After passing this village, continue on the winding road through the area known as the Cretan Riviera, with its spectacular views of the coast to the north, and of the mountains to the east.
43 km - **Sfaka**. Take a detour from here down the dirt road to the left.
50 km - **Mohlos**. A tiny, isolated fishing village with tavernas and rooms to rent. There are Minoan ruins here and on the islands of Psira and Mohlos (see **A-Z**) just across the bay. Return to Sfaka and rejoin the main road heading east in the direction of Sitia.
74 km - **Khamezi**. Visit the remains of an oval-shaped Minoan building, the original function of which has aroused some controversy. Khamezi is also notable as the probable birthplace of the 17thC Cretan writer, Vincent Kornaros, author of the great epic poem, *Erotokritos*. There is a small museum of antiquities just outside the village.
120 km - **Sitia** (see **BEACHES**). A modern harbour town with a population of 6000. There are tavernas along the seafront and a sandy beach. The town also contains two small museums and the remains of a Venetian fort. Continue on the eastern road out of Sitia and turn off to the left after 14 km.
137 km - **Moni Toplou** (see **A-Z**). This fortified 17thC monastery played a major role in various Cretan resistance movements and occupies a strategic position on its high plateau. There are some beautiful icons to be seen in the church. Return to the main road (3 km) and carry on in an easterly direction.
147 km - **Palekastro**. Attractively set amongst olive groves with a beach nearby. It is a 20 min walk from here to the ruins of an ancient Minoan city, the largest ever found, which is likely to be of more interest to the dedicated archeologist than the casual visitor. Take the road north out of Palekastro, continuing straight on at the fork after 6 km. Turn right soon afterwards.

155 km - Vai (see **BEACHES**). The beach here is famous for its forest of palm trees and tropical atmosphere, but it does get very crowded. Take the road back to Sitia via Palekastro (29 km) and then follow the Ierapetra road south through the villages of Piskokefalo and Maronia.
195 km - Epano Episkopi. Stop in this pleasant market centre at the base of the White Mountains for a coffee and a stroll before continuing on the road south. Turn left just before Agios Georgios.
200 km - Nea Praisos. Near the village there are a few remains of an ancient Minoan city which was the last stronghold of the Minoan culture. Rejoin the National road going south and take a left turn at the fork about 6 km further on.
211 km - Etia. Take a look at the fine examples of aristocratic Venetian residences before returning to the main road and heading south along the coastal road.
236 km - Ierapetra (see **BEACHES, A-Z**). The largest town on the south coast has a wonderful long, sandy beach to the west. Leaving town, take the Agios Nikolaos road northwards.
248 km - Vasiliki. This pretty village is the site of a small pre-Minoan settlement dating from c.2500 BC, making it the oldest-known dwelling of any size. The site has given its name to Vasiliki ware, a distinctive type of semi-lustrous pottery found here. Return north to Agios Nikolaos (24 km) along the same road on which you came.

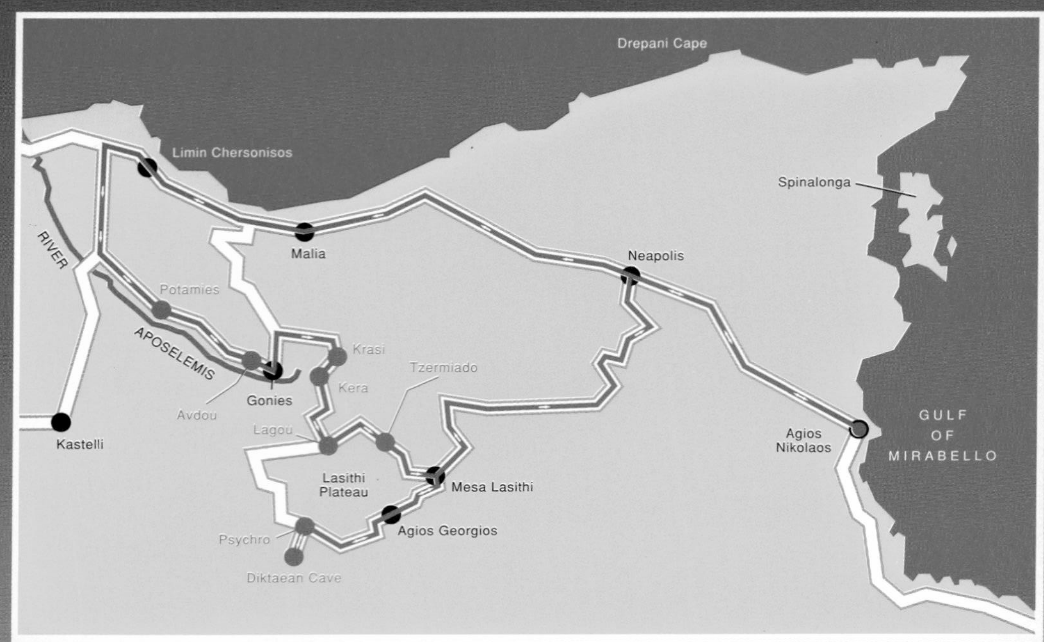
Drepani Cape
Limin Chersonisos
Spinalonga
Malia
Neapolis
RIVER
Potamies
APOSELEMIS
Krasi
Tzermiado
Kera
Gonies
Avdou
Kastelli
Lagou
Lasithi Plateau
Mesa Lasithi
Agios Georgios
Psychro
Diktaean Cave
Agios Nikolaos
GULF OF MIRABELLO

Excursion 2

133 km. *One-day round trip to the Lasithi Plateau (see* **A-Z***) in the Dikti Mountains, taking in the villages of Potamies, Avdou, Krasi, Tzermiado and Psychro, and visiting the famous Diktaean Cave.*

From Agios Nikolaos take the main north-west road towards Heraklion. Pass through the bustling resort of Malia (see **HERAKLION - BEACHES**) 32 km on, and then turn left (inland) after a further 12 km, just past Limin Chersonisos. Follow the road for 6 km before taking the left-hand fork leading through the green valley of the River Aposelemis. Turn left onto a side road after 5 km.

55 km - **Potamies**. Just before entering the village, visit the deserted monastery of Panagia Gouverniotissa which lies off to the left. It is decorated with 14thC frescoes. The Byzantine church of Christos, within the village itself, has more frescoes dating from the 14th-15thC (you may have to ask in the village for keys). Continue in the same direction for another 5 km.

60 km - **Avdou**. There are more churches of interest in and around this unspoilt village, including Agios Antonios, Agios Georgios and Agios Konstantinos (1 km to the south west), all of which have beautiful 14th-15thC frescoes. Carry on from here past the village of Gonies, to the fork in the road about 4 km on. Turn right here and follow the road as it begins to wind up the steep mountainside.

67 km - **Krasi**. An attractive village with huge, ancient plane trees.

70 km - **Kera**. Just before the village drive down to the monastery of Panagia Kera - also known as Kardiotissa - which has interesting architectural features and some well-preserved Byzantine frescoes which have only recently been uncovered (0900-1500 Mon.-Sat., 0900-1400 Sun.). The views of the Lasithi Mountains are excellent from here (you can even see Heraklion, with the sea beyond, in the distance). Pass through the village and keep following the road as it climbs yet higher still. Soon you will catch sight of the plateau with its windmills and perfectly-patterned fields surrounded by a ring of mountains.

76 km - **Lagou**. The first village you come to on the plain. Turn left here and drive around the rim of the plateau in a clockwise direction.

79 km - **Tzermiado**. The starting point for a climb up the peak of Karphi (1100 m) where there are a few traces of an isolated Minoan

and post-Minoan settlement. The views are rewarding, both of the plateau and of the Bay of Malia, but the ascent is steep in places and involves a round trip of over two hours. North east of the village there is also the Trapeza Cave, a Neolithic burial site. Carry on round the plain in the same direction until you reach the south-western side.

91 km - **Psychro**. The principal village of the plateau. A road leads from here up to the famous Diktaean Cave (see **Myths and Legends, A-Z).** It is a 20 min walk from the car park at the end of the road to the cave entrance (0800-1700; small admission fee; guides available at extra cost). Take care inside as it can be slippery underfoot (you should have suitable footwear, warm clothing and a torch). From Psychro, return along the road you came on, going in an easterly direction, and pass through Agios Georgios where there is a small Folklore Museum. Keep going until you reach Mesa Lasithi where you leave the plateau on the road to Neapolis and return to Agios Nikolaos (42 km).

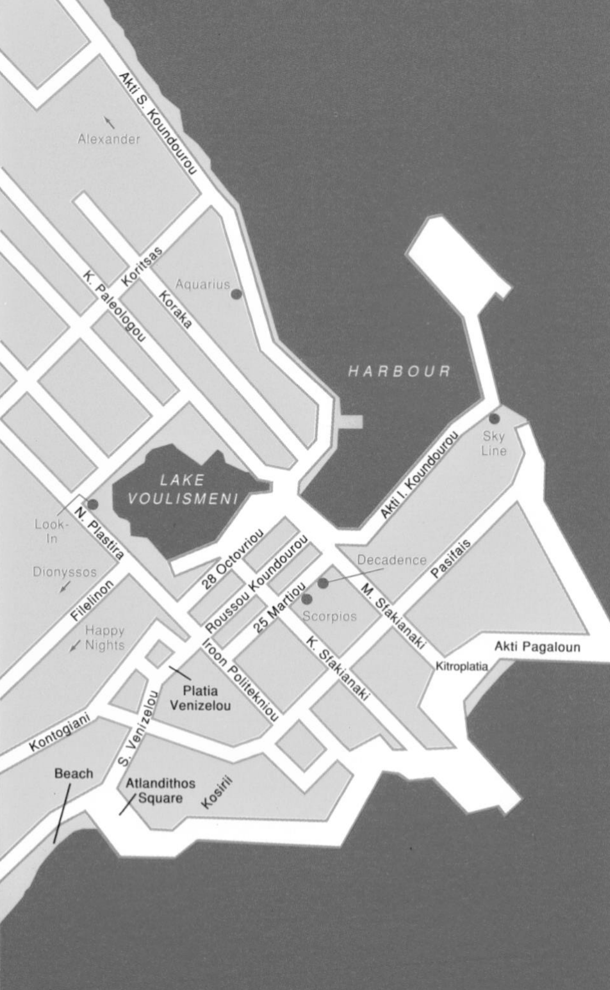

Akti S. Koundourou
Alexander
Koritsas
K. Paleologou
Koraka
Aquarius
HARBOUR
Sky Line
LAKE VOULISMENI
Akti I. Koundourou
Look-In
N. Plastira
28 Octovriou
Roussou Koundourou
Decadence
Pasifais
Dionyssos
Filelinon
25 Martiou
Scorpios
M. Sfakianaki
Happy Nights
Iroon Politekniou
K. Sfakianaki
Akti Pagaloun
Kitroplatia
Platia Venizelou
S. Venizelou
Kontogiani
Beach
Atlandithos Square
Kosirii

Nightlife

See **Opening Times.**

SCORPIOS 25 Martiou St.
Just up from the harbour. • Moderate.
A popular disco which tends to get extremely crowded in the height of the season.

DECADENCE 25 Martiou St.
Near the Scorpios disco (see above). • Moderate.
Trendy bar with a young clientele. Good music.

LOOK-IN N. Plastira St.
West of the lake. • Moderate.
Atmospheric bar with good pop music.

AQUARIUS Akti S. Koundourou.
West of the harbour on the road to Ammoudi. • Moderate.
Pleasant waterside bar where the drinks cost around 500 Drs.

SKY LINE Akti I. Koundourou.
On the quayside. • Expensive.
Fashionable disco with a good selection of music.

ALEXANDER Ammoudi.
On the promontory past the beach. • Moderate.
Excellent atmosphere and reasonable prices. Features different types of music - occasionally bouzouki.

DIONYSSOS Road to Heraklion.
Just outside town. • Moderate.
Specializes in bouzouki *and Cretan music. Authentic atmosphere.*

HAPPY NIGHTS Road to Kritsa.
5 km from Agios Nikolaos. • Moderate.
One of the best dance spots in the area. Great fun.

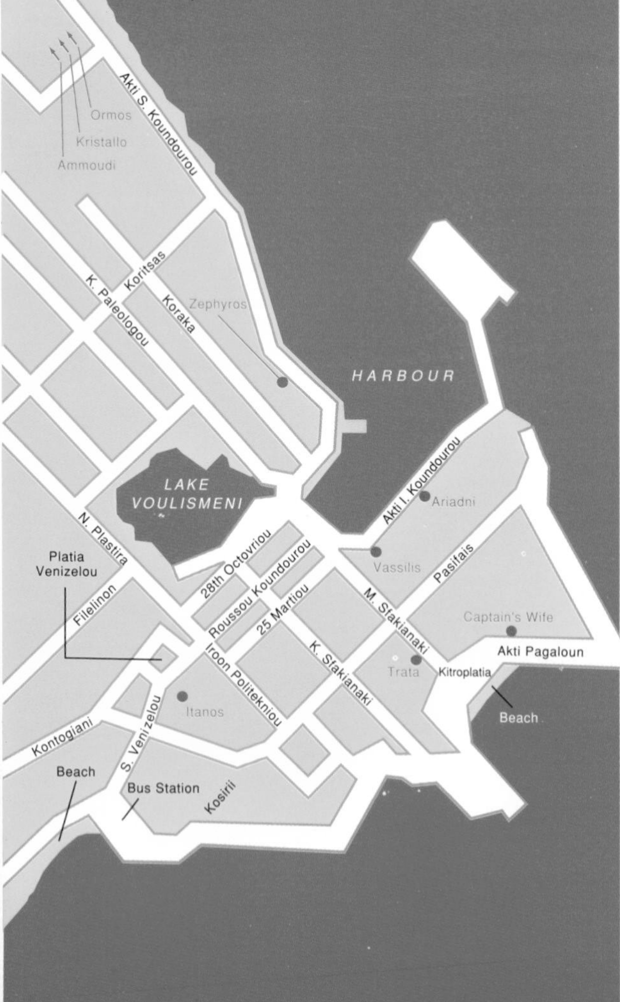

Akti S. Koundourou
Ormos
Kristallo
Ammoudi
Koritsas
K. Paleologou
Koraka
Zephyros
HARBOUR
LAKE
VOULISMENI
Akti I. Koundourou
Ariadni
N. Plastira
Platia
Venizelou
28th Octovriou
Roussou Koundourou
Vassilis
Pasifais
Filelinon
25 Martiou
M. Stakianaki
Captain's Wife
Akti Pagaloun
Iroon Politekniou
K. Sfakianaki
Trata
Kitroplatia
Itanos
Beach
S. Venizelou
Kontogiani
Beach
Bus Station
Kosirii

Restaurants

ORMOS Ammoudi.
•Lunchtimes and evenings. On the promontory past the beach.
•Expensive.
First-class restaurant with Greek and 'international' menu. Bouzouki *music.*

KRISTALLO between Elounda and Agios Nikolaos.
•Open all day. Near the Mirabello Hotel. •Expensive.
Traditional restaurant featuring Syrtos *dancing (see* **Folk Dancing**).

ZEPHYROS Akti S. Koundourou.
•Lunchtimes and evenings. On the seafront. •Moderate.
Popular with tourists who come to sample good local cuisine.

ITANOS Kyprou St. 1.
•Lunchtimes and evenings. Near the central square. •Cheap.
Family atmosphere in this terraced restaurant. Tasty Greek dishes.

TRATA Mihali Sfakianaki St. 14.
•Lunchtimes and evenings. Near the seafront. •Moderate.
Well known for its superb fish dishes.

AMMOUDI Ammoudi.
•Evenings. 10 min from town centre at the beach. •Moderate.
Waterfront taverna serving excellent fish and seafood.

CAPTAIN'S WIFE Kitroplatia.
•Lunchtimes and evenings. Near the waterfront. •Moderate.
Friendly, modern taverna specializing in Cretan cuisine.

ARIADNI Akti I. Koundourou St.
•Lunchtimes and evenings. Beside the harbour. •Expensive.
Family-run establishment offering quality dishes. Popular with tourists.

VASSILIS Akti I. Koundourou St.
•Lunchtimes and evenings. Near the harbour. •Moderate.
Self-service joint for those hankering for fast food.

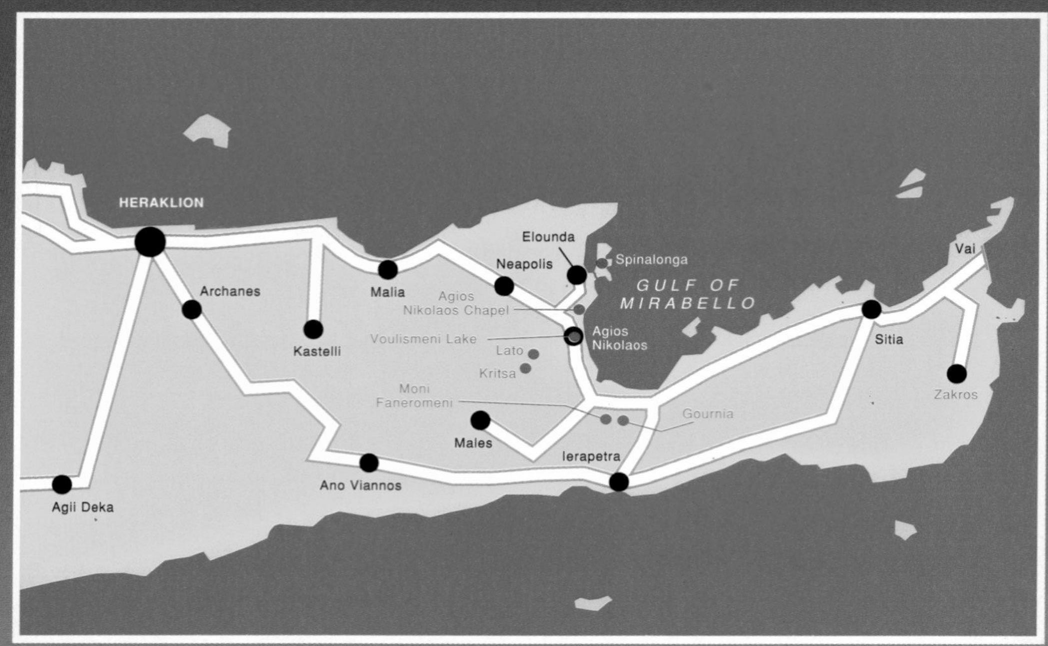
HERAKLION
Archanes
Kastelli
Malia
Neapolis
Elounda
Spinalonga
GULF OF
MIRABELLO
Agios
Nikolaos Chapel
Voulismeni Lake
Agios
Nikolaos
Lato
Kritsa
Moni
Faneromeni
Gournia
Males
Ierapetra
Ano Viannos
Agii Deka
Sitia
Vai
Zakros

VOULISMENI LAKE

Off the harbour in Agios Nikolaos.
A so-called 'bottomless' lake which is actually over 60 m deep and is connected to the outer harbour by a small canal traversed by a little bridge.

AGIOS NIKOLAOS CHAPEL

• Check with tourist office for opening times. On the road to Elounda.
8th or 9thC chapel, dedicated to the patron saint of mariners, from which the town derived its name. Interesting frescoes.

SPINALONGA ISLAND

Off Elounda. Regular boat trips from Agios Nikolaos and Elounda.
Island fortress which served as a leper colony earlier this century. See **A-Z**.

KRITSA

11 km south west of Agios Nikolaos. Local bus hourly 0630-1930.
Large, picturesque village well known as a handicrafts centre. See **A-Z**.

LATO

4 km from Kritsa along a well-signposted track.
Doric remains from 5th-3rdC BC. Magnificent views of the sea and mountains.

ZAKROS

• 0830-1500. 7 km east of Sitia. Bus from Sitia 1100, 1430. • 300 Drs.
The ruins of a Minoan palace, discovered in 1962, which have remained largely undisturbed since it was deserted c.1450 BC. See **A-Z**.

GOURNIA

• 0830-1500 Tues.-Sun. 19 km south east of Agios Nikolaos. Bus to Ierapetra hourly.
Well-preserved remains of a Minoan town. See **A-Z**.

MONI FANEROMENI

• Mornings. East of Agios Nikolaos near Gournia. Bus hourly, then steep climb.
Byzantine convent built around a miraculous grotto. Good views of the Gulf.

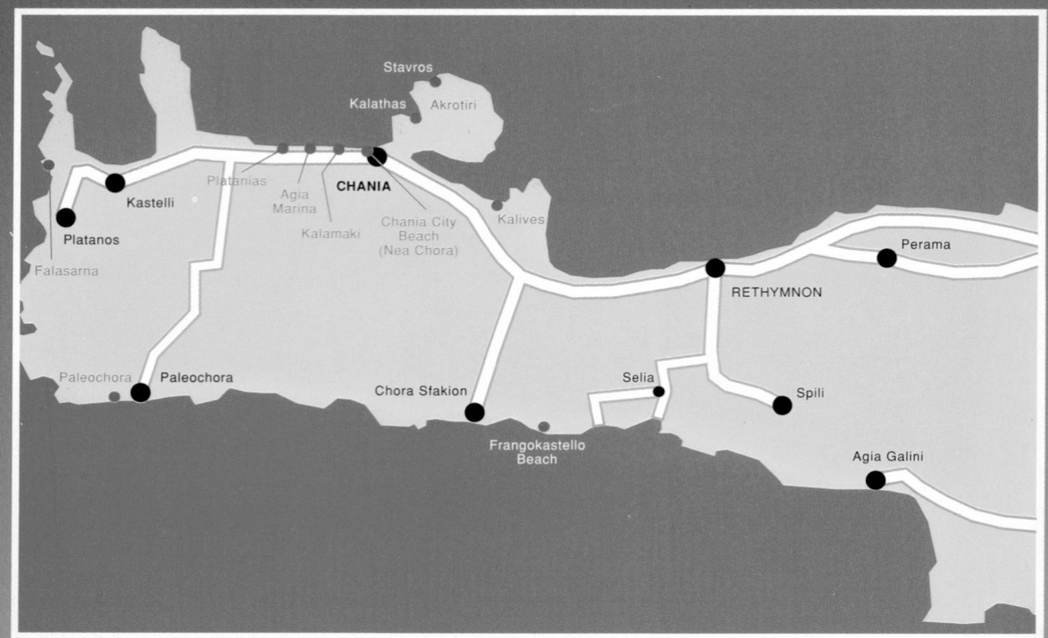
Stavros
Kalathas
Akrotiri
Platanias
Agia Marina
CHANIA
Kastelli
Platanos
Kalamaki
Chania City Beach (Nea Chora)
Kalives
Falasarna
Perama
RETHYMNON
Paleochora
Paleochora
Chora Sfakion
Selia
Spili
Frangokastello Beach
Agia Galini

Beaches

AGIA MARINA
8 km west of Chania. Local bus.
A long, sandy beach with outcrops of rocks. Water sport facilities.

KALAMAKI
5 km west of Chania. Blue city bus.
Sheltered, sandy beach with shallow waters popular for swimming.

CHANIA CITY BEACH (NEA CHORA)
10 min walk from the harbour.
A long, crowded, sandy beach with plenty of amenities.

PLATANIAS
10 km west of Chania.
Popular stretch of grey sand and shingle. Exposed in places.

AKROTIRI
12 km and 16 km north east of Chania. Bus from Chania.
Excellent sandy beaches at Kalathas and Stavros on the peninsula.

KALIVES
20 km east of Chania and just west of Kalives village.
Long, sandy beach beside an unspoilt village with tavernas and places to stay.

FRANGOKASTELLO
12 km east of Chora Sfakion. Bus from Chania daily (summer).
Lovely sandy beach beneath the castle ruins. Clear, shallow water. *See* **A-Z**.

FALASARNA
59 km west of Chania. Car, or bus to Platanos then 5 km hike.
Superb sweep of golden sand in a sheltered bay.

PALEOCHORA
80 km south west of Chania. Bus daily (takes 2 hr).
Magnificent tree-lined sand and shingle beaches on either side of the resort.

Excursion

86 km. *One-day excursion to the biggest natural canyon in Europe, a designated national park where you walk (only in summer) the 18 km from the Omalos Plateau down to the sea at Agia Roumeli (5-6 hr), experiencing some dramatic scenery and glimpsing the areas's abundant flora and fauna. You should equip yourself with suitable footwear and protection from the sun. Water and toilet facilities are available en route. Organized bus and boat trips leave from Chania. See* **Samaria Gorge.**

Take the main road to the west and turn off to the left after 1.5 km to cross the plain, with its deliciously-scented orange groves. Pass through the village of Aghia and take the left-hand fork in the road just before Alikianos, going in a south-easterly direction towards Meskla.
15.5 km - Fournes. Turn off the Meskla road and take the road on the left heading due south.
24.5 km - Lakki. A pretty mountain village with superb views of the White Mountains (Lefka Ori). Keep going south and you enter the Omalos Plateau (1080 m) at its south-west corner. Carry on through the village of Omalos, ignoring the right-hand fork in the road leading round the western edge of the plateau.
43 km - Xyloskalo (Wooden Staircase). The starting point of the walk. There is a tourist centre with a café and limited accommodation for overnight stays (book through NTOG offices - see **Tourist Information**). Descend the steep (1000 m) wooden staircase and then the stepped path to the foot of the upper gorge. The tiny chapel of Agios Nikolaos stands amid the tall cypresses about 2 km on. From here it takes around an hour to reach the small abandoned hamlet of Samaria where you can visit the Byzantine church of Ossia Maria. The path now follows the river bed, crossing and recrossing it until it gets to the towering rock faces of the Sideroportes (Iron Gates), marking the gorge's narrowest point (4 m). From now on the path descends more gently, through wild, beautiful vegetation, and starts to open out as it approaches the old deserted village of Agia Roumeli, and then the sea. The last 2 km stretch of the walk takes you to Agia Roumeli's modern coastal counterpart which has an attractive pebble beach (have a well-earned swim) and plenty of tavernas. Boats depart from here to Chora Sfakion (see **Sfakia**).

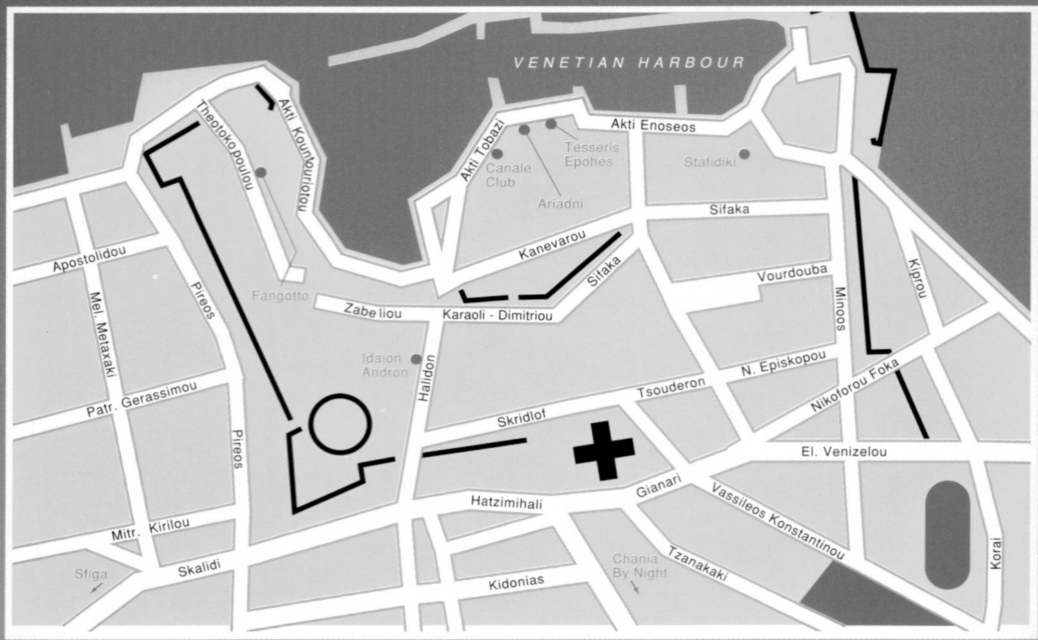
VENETIAN HARBOUR
Akti Enoseos
Akti Tobazi
Akti Kountouriotou
Theotokopoulou
Canale Club
Tesseris Epohes
Ariadni
Stafidiki
Fangotto
Sifaka
Kanevarou
Sifaka
Vourdouba
Minoos
Kiprou
Zabeliou
Karaoli - Dimitriou
Idaion Andron
Halidon
Apostolidou
Pireos
Mel. Metaxaki
Patr. Gerassimou
Pireos
N. Episkopou
Tsouderon
Nikoforou Foka
Skridlof
El. Venizelou
Gianari
Hatzimihali
Vassileos Konstantinou
Mitr. Kirilou
Skalidi
Sfiga
Kidonias
Chania By Night
Tzanakaki
Korai

Nightlife

See **Opening Times.**

FANGOTTO Angelou St. 16, Chania.
Behind the Naval Museum to the west of the old port. •Moderate.
Small, friendly jazz bar with a piano. Occasional performances by live bands.

STAFIDIKI Kalergon St. 11, Chania.
South of the outer harbour. •Moderate.
Elegant establishment with music to suit all tastes.

IDAION ANDRON Halidon St., Chania.
Next to the Archeological Museum. •Expensive.
Friendly, open-air bar. Good selection of music.

ARIADNI Akti Tobazi 19, Chania.
In the old port. •Expensive.
Air-conditioned disco with modern decor.

TESSERIS EPOHES (FOUR SEASONS) Akti Tobazi 26, Chania.
In the old port. •Expensive.
Pleasant waterside bar serving delicious cocktails. Good selection of jazz.

CANALE CLUB Akti Tobazi, Chania.
On the quay at the old port. Free boat across harbour. •Moderate.
Considered to be the best disco in Chania. Beautiful location.

CHANIA BY NIGHT Road to Soudha.
8 km east of Chania. Taxi or car. •Expensive.
Best bouzouki *bar in the area. Cabarets and folk dancing (see* **A-Z***).*

SFIGA Maleme.
17 km west of Chania. Past the Symposio restaurant just west of Maleme. •Moderate.
First-rate disco with a swimming pool. Snacks available.

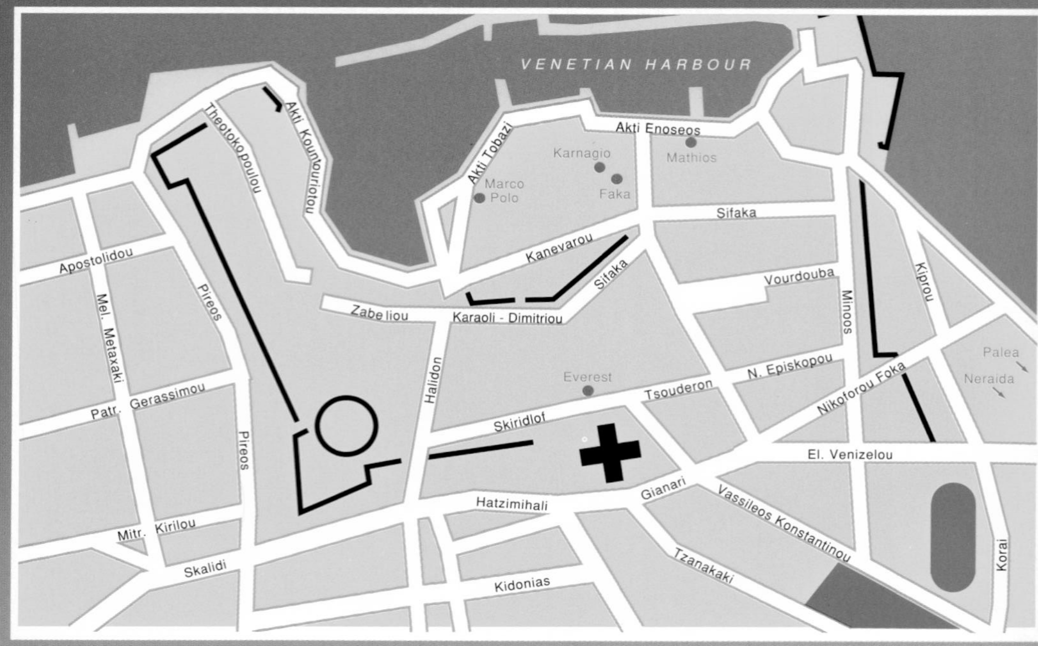

VENETIAN HARBOUR
Akti Enoseos
Mathios
Karnagio
Faka
Akti Tobazi
Marco Polo
Theotokopoulou
Akti Kountouriotou
Sifaka
Kanevarou
Sifaka
Vourdouba
Minoos
Kiprou
Apostolidou
Pireos
Zabeliou
Karaoli - Dimitriou
Mel. Metaxaki
Everest
Palea
Neraida
N. Episkopou
Tsouderon
Nikoforou Foka
Halidon
Patr. Gerassimou
Skiridlof
Pireos
El. Venizelou
Gianari
Vassileos Konstantinou
Hatzimihali
Mitr. Kirilou
Skalidi
Kidonias
Tzanakaki
Korai

Restaurants

NERAIDA Akrotiriou Av 119.
•Evenings. 4 km from Chania on the road to Akrotiri. Taxi. •Expensive.
Elegant restaurant with a veranda overlooking the old quarter. Mainly serves fish dishes.

KARNAGIO Katehaki Sq 8, Chania.
•Lunchtimes and evenings. By the old port. •Moderate.
The best taverna in Chania. Terrace on the square, friendly atmosphere and first-class service.

MARCO POLO Off Akti Tobazi, Chania.
•Lunchtimes and evenings. By the old port behind the Mosque of the Janissaries. •Moderate.
Excellent restaurant offering fresh fish and Greek specialities.

MATHIOS Akti Enoseos 3, Chania.
•Lunchtimes and evenings. In the old port. •Moderate.
Pleasant taverna with a friendly atmosphere. A good place to sample tasty local dishes.

FAKA Archoleon St. 15, Chania.
•Lunchtimes and evenings (summer). In the old port behind the harbour police office. •Moderate.
Informal restaurant with good service, picturesque surroundings and delicious food.

PALEA Evangelistrias St., Chania.
•Daily. In the Halepa quarter. Taxi. •Moderate.
Friendly atmosphere and superb fresh-fish dishes in this taverna owned by Mr Marinakis.

EVEREST Tsouderon St. 41, Chania.
•Lunchtimes and evenings. Near the minaret. •Cheap.
Greek fast-food restaurant for those in a hurry. Try the souvlakis.

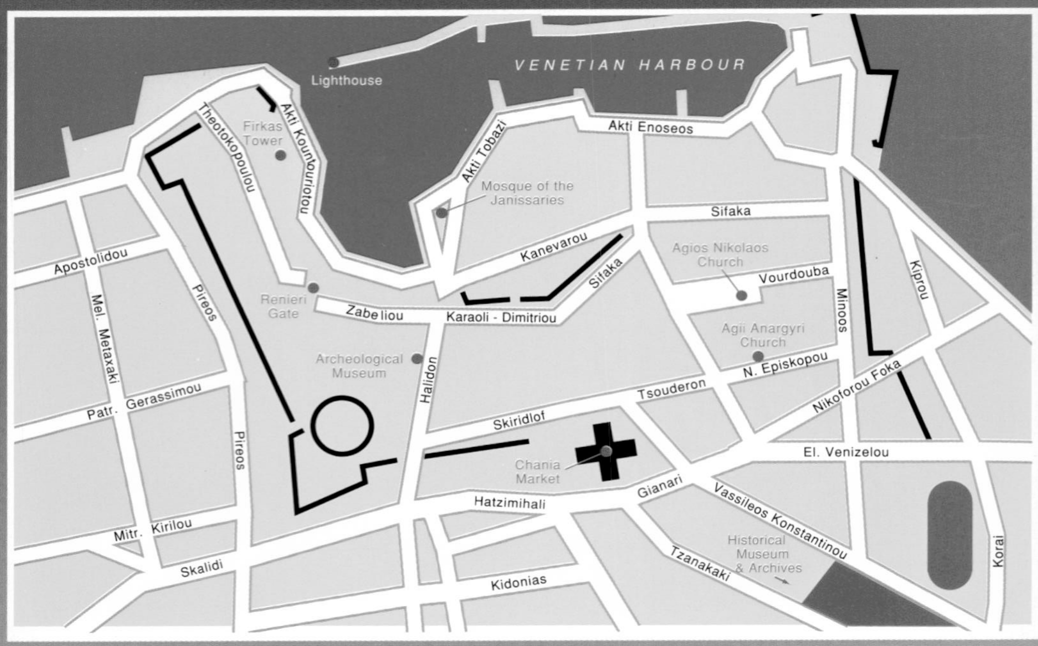

VENETIAN HARBOUR
Lighthouse
Firkas Tower
Theotokopoulou
Akti Kountouriotou
Akti Tobazi
Mosque of the Janissaries
Akti Enoseos
Sifaka
Kanevarou
Sifaka
Agios Nikolaos Church
Vourdouba
Minoos
Kiprou
Apostolidou
Pireos
Renieri Gate
Zabeliou
Karaoli - Dimitriou
Agii Anargyri Church
N. Episkopou
Mel. Metaxaki
Archeological Museum
Halidon
Tsouderon
Nikoforou Foka
Patr. Gerassimou
Skiridlof
El. Venizelou
Pireos
Chania Market
Gianari
Hatzimihali
Vassileos Konstantinou
Mitr. Kirilou
Historical Museum & Archives
Skalidi
Tzanakaki
Kidonias
Korai

What to See

OLD CITY, HARBOUR & LIGHTHOUSE
The chief interest and charm of Chania lies in the Venetian harbour, with its lighthouse, and in the old quarter with its picturesque squares and fountains, handsome buildings and waterfront cafés.

FIRKAS TOWER West of the outer harbour.
Houses the town's Naval Museum. The courtyard is used for theatrical and musical performances during summer.

RENIERI GATE Moshon St.
Elegant archway embellished with a coat of arms and a 17thC inscription.

MOSQUE OF THE JANISSARIES Harbour front.
17thC restored mosque. Houses the NTOG office (see **Tourist Information***)*

AGIOS NIKOLAOS CHURCH Splanzia quarter.
Converted by the Turks in the 17thC when it was renamed after Sultan Ibrahim. A fine minaret stands beside the Greek Orthodox campanile.

AGII ANARGYRI CHURCH Splanzia quarter.
Orthodox church containing some splendid Byzantine frescoes and icons.

CHANIA MARKET Hatzimihali St./Tsouderon St.
Built in the shape of a cross, this bustling covered market has stalls selling all kinds of regional food and crafts. See **Chania**.

ARCHEOLOGICAL MUSEUM Halidon St.
•0800-1900 Tues.-Fri., 1230-1900 Mon., 0830-1530 Sat.-Sun.
Housed in the restored Venetian church of Agios Frangiskos. Minoan pottery, sarcophagi, inscribed tablets, classical sculptures and mosaics. See **A-Z**.

HISTORICAL MUSEUM & ARCHIVES Sfakianaki St. 20.
•0900-1300, 1500-1730 Mon.-Fri. Near the public gardens.
Archive material and relics relating to the Cretan struggle for independence against the Turks and the life of the statesman, Eleftherios Venizelos (see **A-Z***). See* **Chania.**

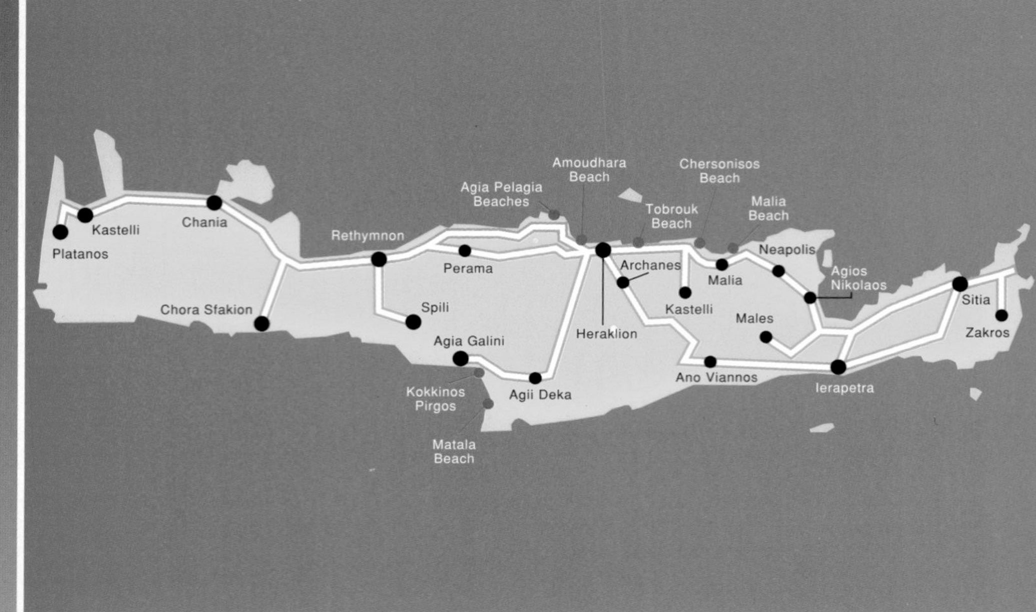

Amoudhara Beach
Chersonisos Beach
Agia Pelagia Beaches
Tobrouk Beach
Malia Beach
Neapolis
Kastelli
Chania
Rethymnon
Archanes
Agios Nikolaos
Platanos
Perama
Malia
Sitia
Spili
Kastelli
Males
Chora Sfakion
Heraklion
Zakros
Agia Galini
Kokkinos Pirgos
Agii Deka
Ano Viannos
Ierapetra
Matala Beach

TOBROUK

7 km east of Heraklion near the airport. Local bus 1 from the city centre.
One of the closest beaches to the capital, making it an extremely popular spot. Tavernas and cold drink stands. Quieter areas further along.

AMOUDHARA

6 km west of Heraklion. Bus from Porta Chania.
Sandy, resort beach which is a bit dirty. You can find more secluded and cleaner spots by walking further west around the bay.

CHERSONISOS

29 km east of Heraklion. Bus from the port.
A small, sandy, and fairly clean beach beside this ancient settlement which is now a busy tourist resort. Nudist bathing in the vicinity (see **Nudism***). See* **A-Z**.

MALIA

37 km east of Heraklion. Bus from the port.
Popular beach with fine sand and clear, shallow water. Plenty of shops, tavernas, discos and cocktail bars in the crowded resort.

AGIA PELAGIA

15 km west of Heraklion. Bus from Porta Chania.
Good beaches of sand, rock and pebble on either side of this up-market resort. Water sport facilities and sheltered waters.

MATALA

75 km south west of Heraklion. Bus from Porta Chania.
Idyllic beach which shelves deeply into the sea at this former hippy haven (now a mainstream tourist development). Underwater remains and lots of caves.

KOKKINOS PIRGOS

73 km south west of Heraklion. Regular bus service from Porta Chania.
Beach stretching west towards Agia Galini (see **EXCURSION 1***). Popular with the area's local inhabitants, but not the most attractive in the region.*

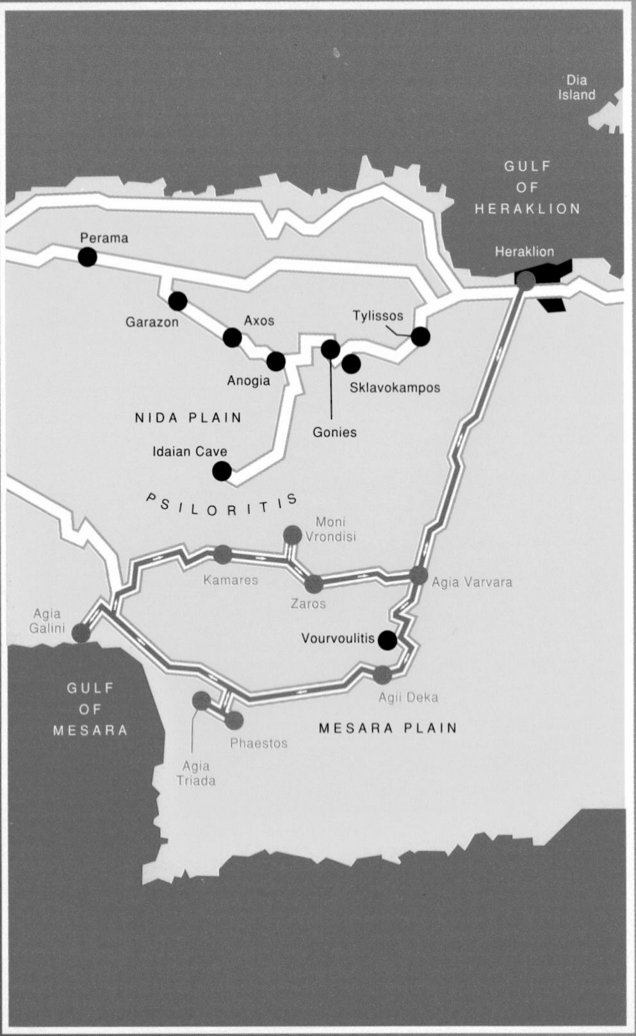

Dia
Island

GULF
OF
HERAKLION

Heraklion

Perama

Garazon

Axos

Tylissos

Anogia

Sklavokampos

NIDA PLAIN

Gonies

Idaian Cave

PSILORITIS

Moni
Vrondisi

Kamares

Zaros

Agia Varvara

Agia
Galini

Vourvoulitis

GULF
OF
MESARA

Agii Deka

MESARA PLAIN

Phaestos

Agia
Triada

Excursion 1

169 km. *One-day excursion to the south taking in the archeological and historic sites of Agii Deka, Gortys, Phaestos, Agia Triada, Kamares, Zaros and Moni Vrondisi.*

Leave the city in a westerly direction through the Porta Chania (Chania Gate). After 2 km turn left onto the Agia Galini road heading south towards the lower eastern slopes of Psiloritis (Mount Ida).
30 km - Agia Varvara (600 m). The main village of the region and generally considered to be the geographic centre of the island. Continue south along the main road as it climbs to its highest point at Vourvoulitis before descending, in a series of hairpin bends, to the Mesara Plain.
45 km - Agii Deka ('Holy Ten'). This is the first village you come to on the fertile plain. Ten Christians were beheaded near here during the Roman persecutions of AD 250 for refusing to abandon their faith (hence the name of the village). A church within the village is dedicated to their memory and a modern chapel just outside is said to contain the martyred saints' tombs. The path going off the road just opposite the chapel leads to Gortys (see **A-Z**), the large, sprawling, poorly-marked site of a Greco-Roman city (0800-1900; 200 Drs). Return to the main road and drive in a westerly direction towards Agia Galini. Turn left after about 16 km.
63 km - Phaestos (see **A-Z**). The site of a Minoan town built by the same workmen as those who constructed Knossos (see **A-Z**). It boasts the best-preserved palace from the Cretan-Minoan period (0800-1900; 350 Drs). The views of the Mesara Plain and the mountains are spectacular. Take the right fork just past the site's car park and drive for 2 km.
65 km - Agia Triada (see **A-Z**). The palace here, which is also set in beautiful countryside, is modest in comparison to those at Phaestos and Knossos (see **A-Z**) and is believed to have been a summer retreat or the residence of a prince (0830-1500; 200 Drs). Return to the main road and turn left.
85 km - Agia Galini. This fishing village now has a rapidly-expanding tourist trade and has lost some of its old charm, but there are interesting caves nearby and numerous tavernas and bars where you can stop for

refreshments. There are two small, crowded beaches accessible by a cliff track if you feel like a swim, although the best beaches lie off to the west. Leaving the village, return along the road by which you entered for several kilometres, then turn left and carry on for another few kilometres before turning right and heading inland towards Psiloritis in the north east.

105 km - **Kamares**. You can climb to the famous Kamares Cave (1520 m), a Minoan sanctuary discovered in 1890, from here but, since the round trip takes nearly eight hours and the ascent is steep, it is not recommended for the casual walker. The cave gave its name to Kamares ware, a fine prehistoric pottery found here. Continue in the same direction for a further 11 km. Turn left and drive north for 3 km.

116 km - **Moni Vrondisi**. A famous 14thC monastery with interesting frescoes and an ornate 15thC Venetian fountain. There are superb views from here. Return along the same route to the main road.

119 km - **Zaros**. A typical, attractive Cretan village containing several ancient churches.

Continue east and you will eventually reach Agia Varvara which you have already passed through. From here return to Heraklion along the route on which you came.

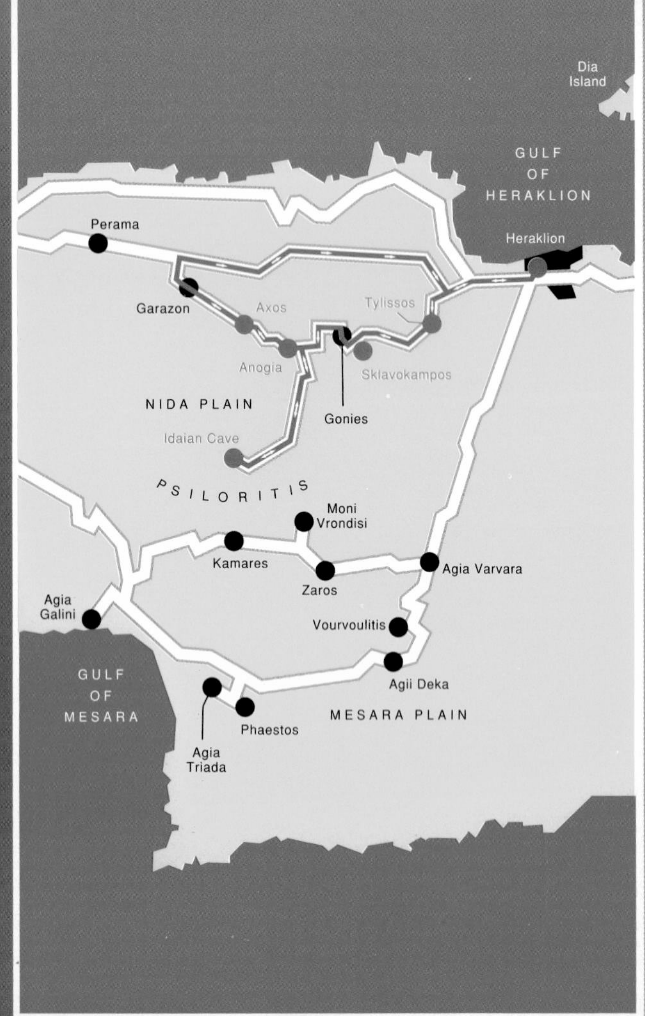

Dia
Island
GULF
OF
HERAKLION
Heraklion
Perama
Garazon
Axos
Tylissos
Anogia
Sklavokampos
NIDA PLAIN
Gonies
Idaian Cave
PSILORITIS
Moni
Vrondisi
Kamares
Zaros
Agia Varvara
Agia
Galini
Vourvoulitis
Agii Deka
GULF
OF
MESARA
Phaestos
MESARA PLAIN
Agia
Triada

Excursion 2

138 km. *One-day excursion to Psiloritis (Mount Ida) and the Idaian Cave, taking in the ancient sites of Tylissos, Sklavokampos and Axos, and the picturesque village of Anogia.*

Take the westerly road out of Heraklion through the Porta Chania. Turn left after 10 km and head along the northern slopes of Psiloritis. The road has numerous bends with sheer drops, so take care.
15 km - **Tylissos**. The ruins of three large Minoan villas here, destroyed between 1450-1400 BC, constitute one of Crete's earliest and most important archeological sites (0830-1500; 200 Drs). Finds from the site are displayed in the Archeological Museum at Heraklion (see **WHAT TO SEE, A-Z**).
20 km - **Sklavokampos**. Excavations of another large Minoan villa. Continue along the same road through the traditional Cretan village of Gonies. Just before the village of Anogia, turn off to the left and drive up the winding road leading to the Nida Plain.
56 km - **Idaian Cave** (see **A-Z**). From the end of the road it is a 20 min walk to the entrance of the cave which, along with the Diktaean Cave (see **AGIOS NIKOLAOS - EXCURSION 2, A-Z**), is famous in Greek mythology as Zeus' birthplace (see **Myths and Legends**). Return down the road you came on and then turn left back onto the main road.
76 km - **Anogia**. The village suffered great damage during the Second World War. It is notable for its brightly-coloured woven goods and folk traditions (see **Best Buys, Ceremonies, Crafts)** and is a popular stopping-off point for organized excursions. Continue in a north-westerly direction.
84 km - **Axos**. Five minutes walk beyond the village (follow the signs) is the site of ancient Axos. Once an important town, there is little to be seen here today, although the Cyclopean walls can still be made out. Finds from the site are housed in Heraklion's Archeological Museum (see **WHAT TO SEE, A-Z**). Visit the village's Byzantine church to see some superb frescoes (those by Ai Yannis are particularly noteworthy) before heading through Garazon to the main Perama/Heraklion road where you should turn right to return to the capital.

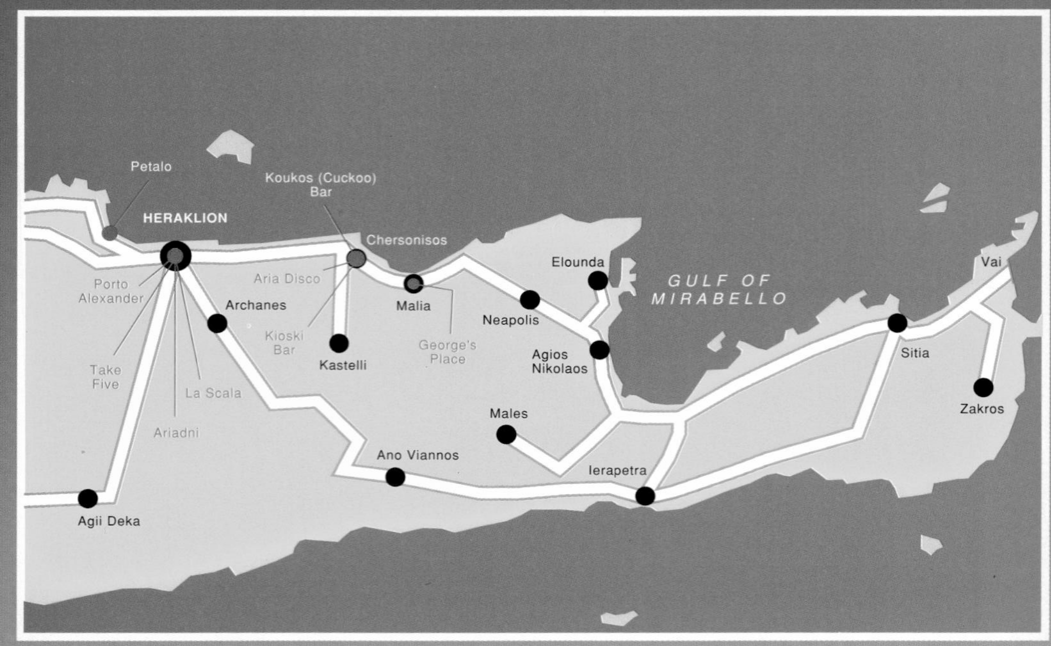
Petalo
Koukos (Cuckoo) Bar
HERAKLION
Chersonisos
Elounda
Vai
GULF OF MIRABELLO
Porto Alexander
Aria Disco
Archanes
Malia
Neapolis
Kioski Bar
Kastelli
George's Place
Agios Nikolaos
Sitia
Take Five
La Scala
Zakros
Males
Ariadni
Ano Viannos
Ierapetra
Agii Deka

Nightlife

See **Opening Times.**

PORTO ALEXANDER Epimenidou St., Heraklion.
Off 25 Avgoustou near the harbour front. •Moderate.
Fashionable disco with a convivial atmosphere.

TAKE FIVE Off Venizelou Sq, Heraklion.
Up from 25 Avgoustou. •Cheap.
Good bar with an excellent choice of pop music.

LA SCALA Bofor St., Heraklion.
Up from the harbour bus station. •Moderate.
The trendiest of Heraklion's discos - good music and decor.

ARIADNI Knossos Av.
5 km south of city centre just before Knossos. Taxi. •Expensive.
Atmospheric nightclub featuring Cretan folk music and dancing (see **A-Z***).*

PETALO Linoperamata.
10 km west of Heraklion. Taxi. •Moderate.
Nightclub serving food. Cretan music, singing and dancing.

KOUKOS (CUCKOO) BAR Chersonisos.
7 km west of Malia. On the seafront. •Expensive.
Pleasant bar with a relaxed atmosphere serving delicious cocktails.

ARIA DISCO Chersonisos.
On the right of the road entering town. •Cheap.
One of the best discos in the area. Excellent music.

KIOSKI BAR 25 Martiou St., Chersonisos.
7 km west of Malia. At the eastern end of the seafront. •Moderate.
Lovely views over sea - an ideal place for a quiet drink.

GEORGE'S PLACE Malia.
On the beach road near the resort. •Moderate.
Friendly bar especially popular with American tourists. Handy for beach.

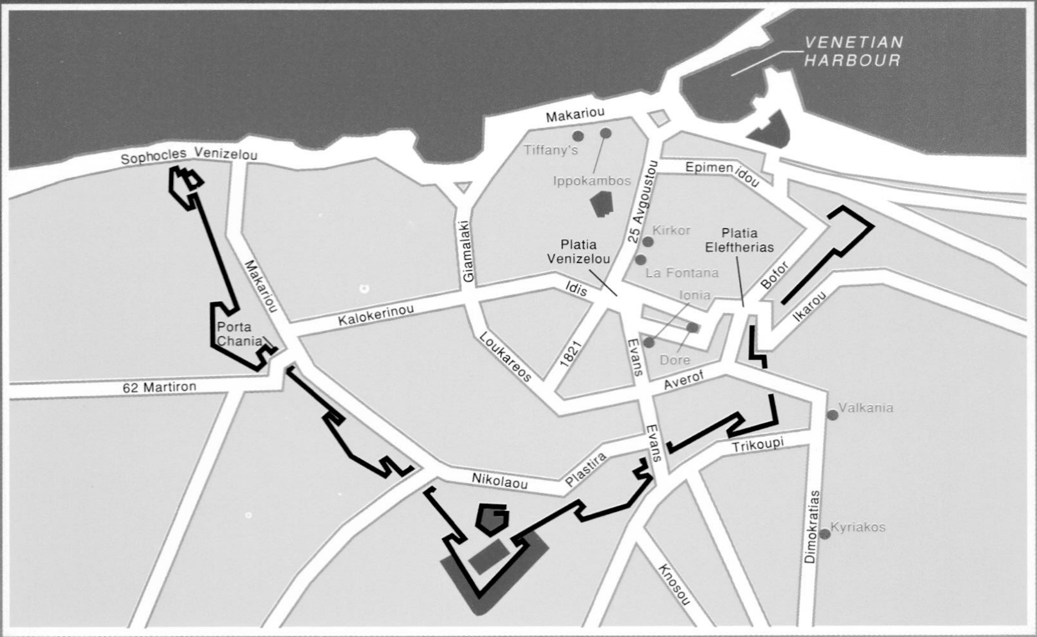

VENETIAN
HARBOUR
Makariou
Tiffany's
Ippokambos
Sophocles Venizelou
Epimenidou
25 Avgoustou
Kirkor
La Fontana
Platia
Venizelou
Platia
Eleftherias
Bofor
Ikarou
Ionia
Dore
Giamalaki
Idis
Kalokerinou
Makariou
Porta
Chania
Loukareos
1821
Evans
Averof
62 Martiron
Valkania
Evans
Trikoupi
Nikolaou
Plastira
Dimokratias
Kyriakos
Knosou

Restaurants

KYRIAKOS Dimokratias St. 45.
• Lunchtimes and evenings Thurs.-Tues. • Expensive.
Elegant restaurant offering a wide-ranging choice of excellent Greek dishes.

DORE Eleftherias Sq.
• Lunchtimes and evenings. Fifth floor and roof, entrance in arcade.
• Expensive.
Pleasant café/restaurant with a piano bar. International cuisine.

TIFFANY'S Heraklion Port.
• 2130. Near the bus station. • Expensive.
Restaurant and piano bar housed in a beautiful Neoclassical building. Superb international cuisine.

IONIA Evans St. 5.
• Evenings. In the town centre. • Moderate.
Cretan-style restaurant offering quality dishes.

VALKANIA Dimokratias Av 11.
• Lunchtimes and evenings. In the town centre. • Moderate.
Excellent restaurant serving a simple Greek cuisine. Popular with locals.

LA FONTANA Venizelou St. 24.
• Lunchtimes and evenings. Near Venizelou Sq. • Moderate.
Modern restaurant mostly appealing to a young clientele. Serves pizzas and pasta dishes.

IPPOKAMBOS Mutsokatis St.
• Evenings. Between the port and the Xenia Hotel. • Moderate.
If you are looking for a drink and snack try the tasty mezedes, *traditionally served with* ouzo, *at this small friendly taverna specializing in seafood.*

KIRKOR Venizelou Sq.
• Lunchtimes and evenings. By the fountain. • Moderate.
A good place to sample a delicious bouyatsa *- a hot cheese pastry sprinkled with sugar.*

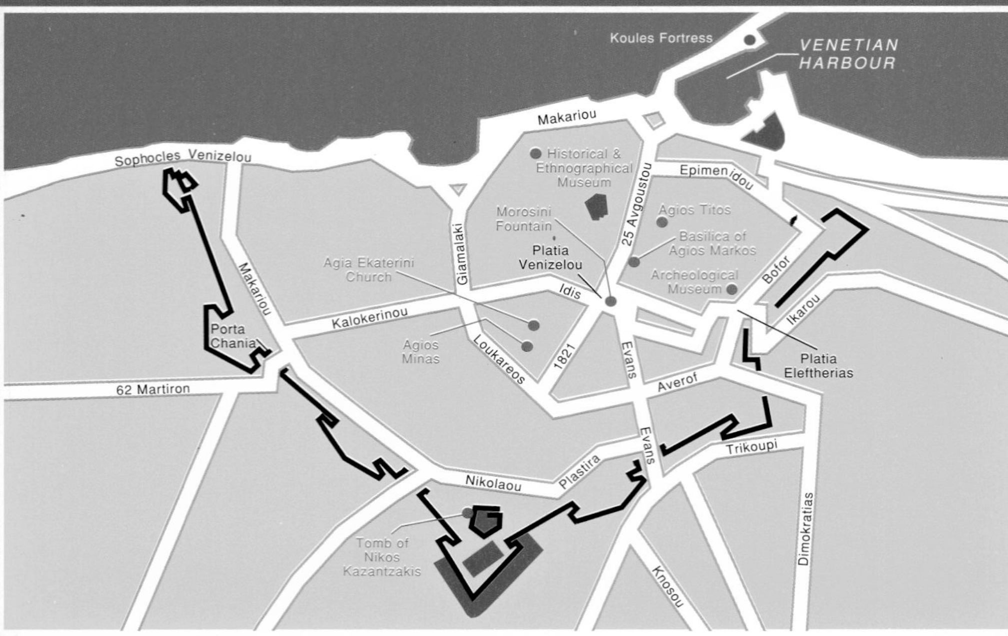
Koules Fortress
VENETIAN HARBOUR
Makariou
Sophocles Venizelou
Historical & Ethnographical Museum
Epimenidou
25 Avgoustou
Agios Titos
Morosini Fountain
Basilica of Agios Markos
Platia Venizelou
Agia Ekaterini Church
Giamalaki
Archeological Museum
Bofor
Idis
Ikarou
Makariou
Kalokerinou
Porta Chania
Agios Minas
Loukareos
1821
Evans
Platia Eleftherias
Averof
62 Martiron
Evans
Trikoupi
Plastira
Nikolaou
Tomb of Nikos Kazantzakis
Dimokratias
Knosou

What to See

ARCHEOLOGICAL MUSEUM Xanthoudidou St.
•0800-1900 Tues.-Sun., 1230-1900 Mon. Off Eleftherias Sq. •500 Drs.
One of Greece's finest museums. See **A-Z.**

HISTORICAL & ETHNOGRAPHICAL MUSEUM Kalokerinou St.
•0900-1700 Mon.-Sat. Opposite the Xenia Hotel. •300 Drs.
Interesting collection of frescoes, sculptures and coins. Visit the reconstructed study of Crete's famous author, Nikos Kazantzakis (see **A-Z***). See* **A-Z**.

TOMB OF NIKOS KAZANTZAKIS Martinengo Bastion.
Imposing tomb of the author of Zorba, *inscribed with the words 'I hope for nothing. I fear nothing. I am free.' See* **Kazantzakis.**

AGIA EKATERINI Agias Ekaterini Sq.
•1000-1300 Mon.-Sat., 1600-1800 Tues., Thurs., Fri. •150 Drs.
16thC church housing the excellent Museum of Religious Art. See **A-Z**.

KOULES FORTRESS Venetian harbour.
•0730-1730 (depending on exhibitions). •200 Drs.
Imposing 16thC Venetian fortress decorated with the Lions of St Mark.

AGIOS TITOS 25 Avgoustou.
•0700-1200, 1700-2000. Near Venizelou Sq.
Rebuilt and restored several times, the church has served the Greek Orthodox, Catholic and Islamic faiths. Contains the skull of St Titus (see **A-Z***).*

BASILICA OF AGIOS MARKOS Venizelou Sq.
Twice damaged by earthquakes, rebuilt by the Venetians and converted into a mosque under the Turks, the church now houses reproductions of frescoes.

MOROSINI FOUNTAIN Venizelou (Fountain) Sq.
Fine Venetian fountain decorated with marble lions and mythological figures.

AGIOS MINAS Agias Ekaterinis Sq.
•0730-1800 daily.
This huge 19thC cathedral dominates the tiny original church beside it.

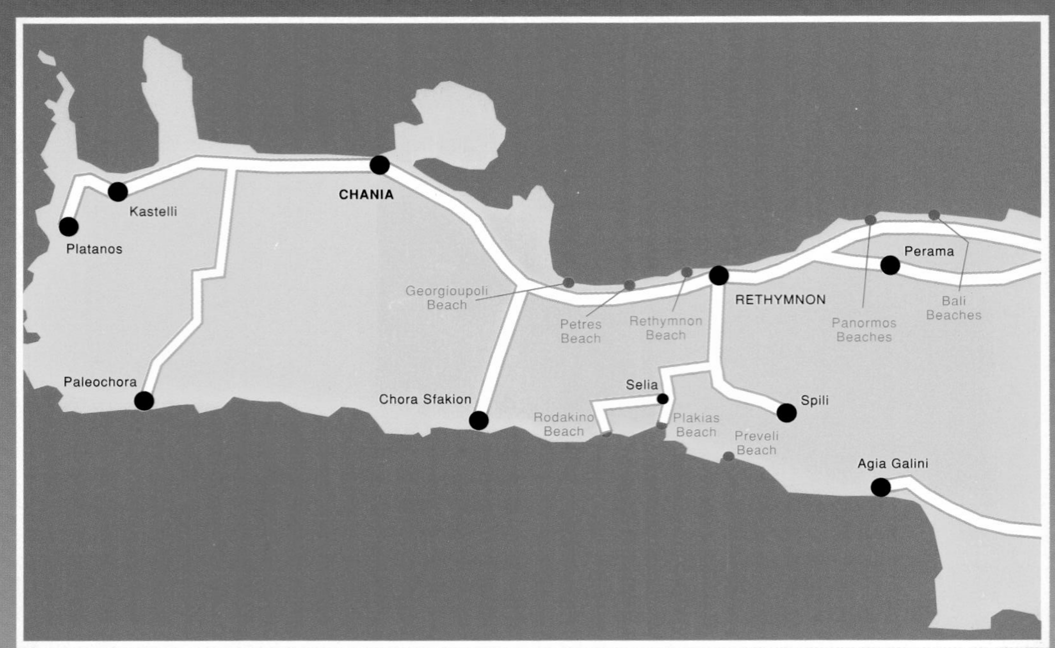
CHANIA
Kastelli
Platanos
Paleochora
Chora Sfakion
Georgioupoli Beach
Petres Beach
Rethymnon Beach
RETHYMNON
Selia
Rodakino Beach
Plakias Beach
Preveli Beach
Spili
Perama
Panormos Beaches
Bali Beaches
Agia Galini

Beaches

RETHYMNON
In front of the resort.
Long, popular stretch of sand with shallow waters safe for swimming.

PETRES
15 km west of Rethymnon. Chania bus to Episkopi turn-off.
Beautiful sandy beach extending from the Petres River to Georgioupoli (see below). There are dangerous currents in places.

GEORGIOUPOLI
27 km west of Rethymnon. Regular bus service.
The other end of the sandy beach that starts at Petres (see above). The shallow waters at this small, pleasant resort are protected by a breakwater.

RODAKINO
45 km south west of Rethymnon and 2 km from Rodakino.
Attractive beach of fine sand and pebble surrounded by rocks and caves.

PLAKIAS
39 km south west of Rethymnon. Regular bus service.
Long, magnificent, but exposed beach stretching between Cape Kakomouri and Cape Stavros at this popular resort. See **EXCURSION**.

BALI
35 km east of Rethymnon. Access from the new road. Bus and by foot.
Three sheltered beaches of sand and pebble set in coves at this attractive little resort at the foot of mountains.

PANORMOS
24 km east of Rethymnon. Access from the new road. Car.
Two small beaches - one of sand, one with rocks and pebbles - at this historic village.

PREVELI
35 km south of Rethymnon. Bus to monastery then 20-30 min walk.
Picturesque, palm-fringed beach beneath the monastery. See **EXCURSION**.

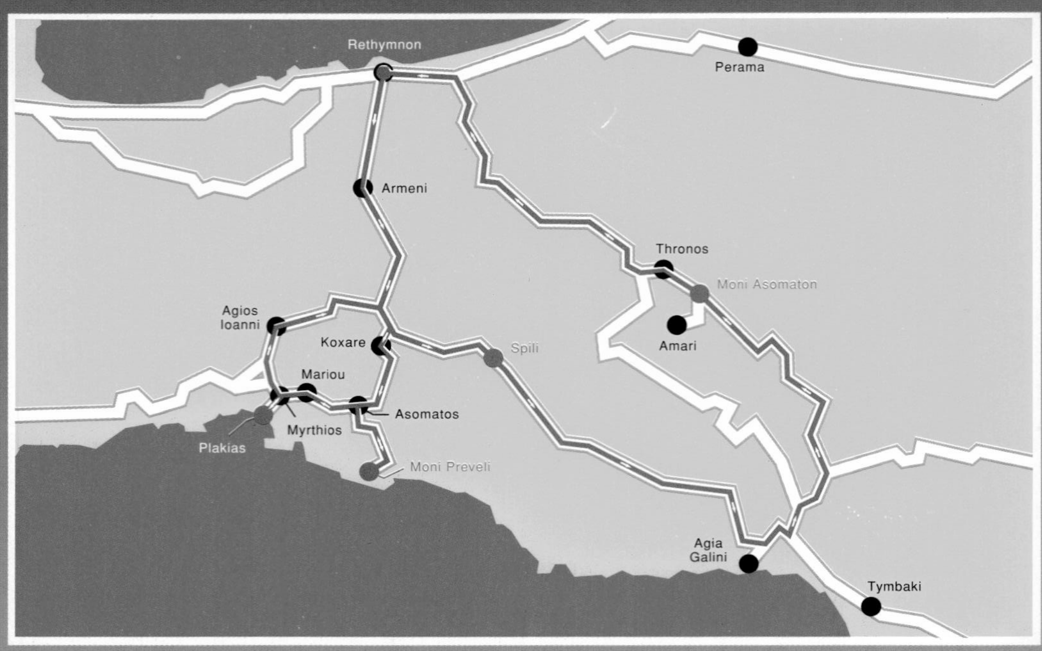
Rethymnon
Perama
Armeni
Thronos
Moni Asomaton
Amari
Agios
Ioanni
Koxare
Spili
Mariou
Asomatos
Myrthios
Plakias
Moni Preveli
Agia
Galini
Tymbaki

Excursion

175.5 km. *One-day excursion to Moni Preveli, Plakias, Spili and Moni Asomaton.*

Take the south road out of Rethymnon heading in the direction of Agia Galini (see **HERAKLION - EXCURSION 1**) and pass through the village of Armeni (9.5 km). Stay on the main road, ignoring the road going off to the left at the next junction, and the one off to the right about 8 km further on. After 1.5 km take the next right turn and follow the road through the village of Koxare towards the Kourtaliotis Gorge (see **A-Z**). Take the first turning to the left at Asomatos and keep going along this road, keeping to the left at the next fork, as it becomes a dirt track and passes the ruins of an old monastery.

35 km - Moni Preveli. 17thC monastery where allied soldiers hid during the Second World War. The church has a small museum and a library, and there are good views of the Libyan Sea. A steep footpath leads down to a popular, palm-fringed beach (see **BEACHES**). Return to Asomatos, turn left, and carry on through the villages of Mariou and Myrthios, then turn left again for the seaside.

55 km - Plakias (see **BEACHES**). This sleepy village, now a small resort, has a good beach with facilities for underwater fishing. Its tavernas serve excellent fresh fish if you feel like stopping for a meal. Return to the main road, turn left and then right onto the road to Agios Ioanni. Turn right 9 km after the village and follow the road for a further 9 km.

80 km - Spili. Stop and explore this beautiful hillside village with its picturesque tree-lined main square, its springs and Venetian fountain, traditional houses and frescoed churches. Keep going in the same direction to Agia Galini (see **HERAKLION - EXCURSION 1**) 29 km on, then take the road to the east heading for Timbaki. Turn left after 5 km and drive towards Amari. Turn right at the fork 1.5 km further on, left after another 4 km, then carry straight on.

139.5 km - Moni Asomaton. This beautiful monastery now houses an agricultural school. Continue north through Thronos, from where there are superb views of the beautiful Amari valley, dotted with hamlets and richly-decorated Byzantine churches. A short climb also takes you to the remains of an acropolis below the ancient site of Syvritos. Carry on northwards to return to Rethymnon (31 km).

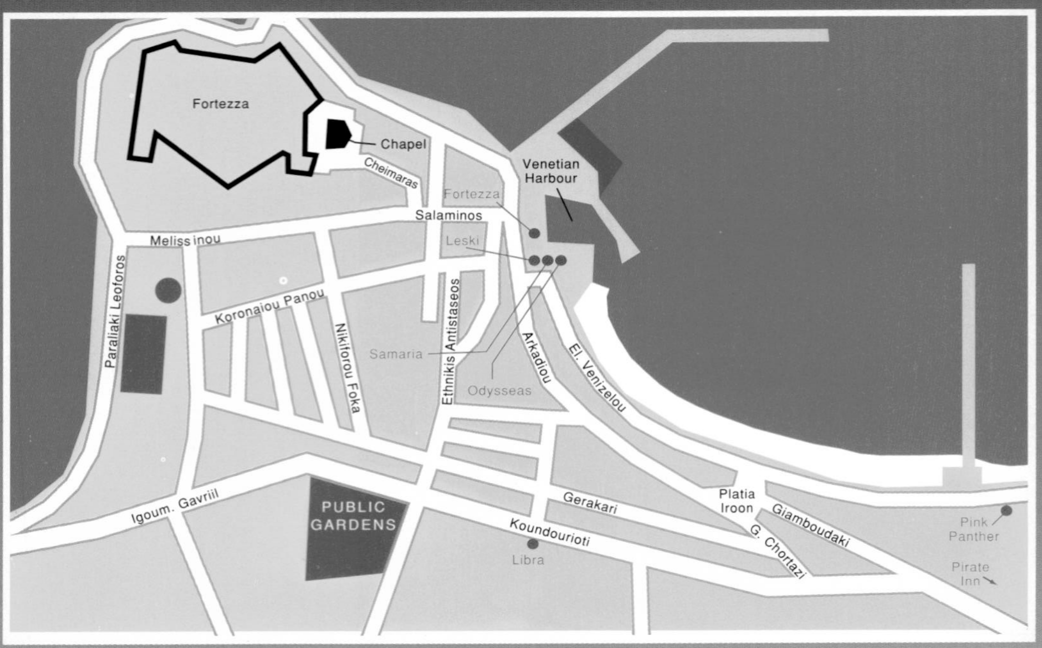

Fortezza
Chapel
Cheimaras
Venetian Harbour
Fortezza
Salaminos
Leski
Meliss inou
Paraliaki Leoforos
Koronaiou Panou
Nikiforou Foka
Samaria
Ethnikis Antistaseos
Odysseas
Arkadiou
El. Venizelou
Platia Iroon
Giamboudaki
G. Chortazi
Gerakari
Koundourioti
Libra
PUBLIC GARDENS
Igoum. Gavriil
Pink Panther
Pirate Inn

Nightlife

See **Opening Times.**

PINK PANTHER Sofokli Venizelou St. 42, Rethymnon.
On the seafront near the Kriti Beach Hotel.
• Cheap.
Small, quiet bar facing the sea. Friendly service. Serves snacks.

FORTEZZA Old port, Rethymnon.
Near the inner harbour.
• Moderate.
Air-conditioned disco popular with young people. Not too big.

LESKI Ioulias Petichaki St. 8, Rethymnon.
Next door to the Samaria (see below).
• Cheap.
Pleasant bar offering good music and dancing. Popular with tourists.

SAMARIA Ioulias Petichaki St. 8, Rethymnon.
Next to the Odysseas (see below).
• Moderate.
Bouzouki *bar with a lively floor show.*

ODYSSEAS Old port, Rethymnon.
Additional entrance off Ioulias Petichaki St.
• Moderate.
Picturesque taverna featuring bouzouki *and Greek dancing. Serves food.*

LIBRA Koundourioti St. 23, Rethymnon.
In the town centre.
• Moderate.
Trendy disco appealing to a young clientele.

PIRATE INN Platanias.
6 km east of Rethymnon just beyond Platanias.
• Moderate.
Modern bar specializing in delicious cocktails.

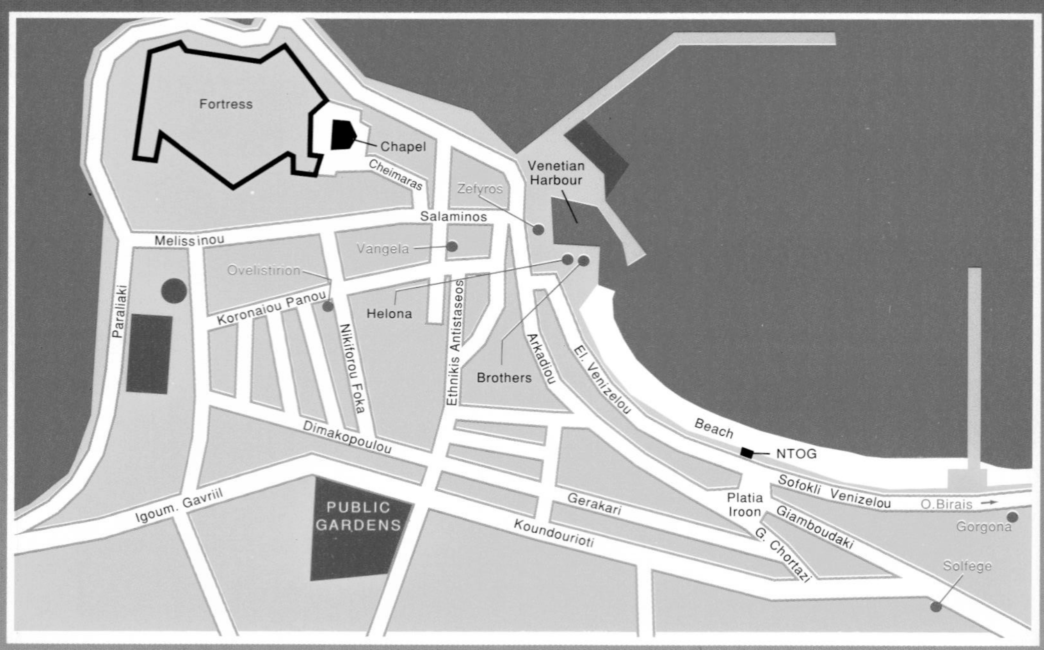
Fortress
Chapel
Cheimaras
Venetian
Harbour
Zefyros
Salaminos
Melissinou
Vangela
Ovelistirion
Koronaiou Panou
Helona
Paraliaki
Nikiforou Foka
Ethnikis Antistaseos
Brothers
Arkadiou
El. Venizelou
Beach
NTOG
Dimakopoulou
Sofokli Venizelou
O.Birais
Gorgona
Platia
Iroon
Giamboudaki
Gerakari
G. Chortazi
Koundourioti
Igoum. Gavriil
PUBLIC
GARDENS
Solfege

Restaurants

O. BIRAIS Sofokli Venizelou St. 62-63.
•Midday-midnight. On the seafront. •Moderate.
Traditional taverna serving well-cooked Greek food. Lively and informal.

GORGONA Papanastasiou St.
•Breakfast time-0200. Corner of Sofokli Venizelou St. opposite the Kriti Beach Hotel. •Expensive
A pleasant restaurant facing the sea. Specializes in Greek-style fish dishes.

HELONA Old port.
•Lunchtimes and evenings. •Moderate.
Friendly taverna serving good seafood in a picturesque setting.

BROTHERS (ADELPHI) Old port.
•Lunchtimes and evenings. •Moderate.
There is aggressive touting for customers to this attractive restaurant serving grilled meat and fish dishes.

OVELISTIRION Nikiforou Foka St. 98.
•Lunchtimes and evenings. Opposite the church of the Annunciation. •Moderate.
Taverna offering the usual range of grilled dishes.

ZEFYROS Old port.
•Lunchtimes and evenings. •Moderate.
Delightful restaurant offering a typical Cretan cuisine.

VANGELA Diogeni-Moskoviti St. 6.
•Lunchtimes and evenings. In the tiny street just behind the Rimondi Fountain. •Moderate.
Charming restaurant serving excellent Greek food.

SOLFEGE Koundourioti St. 153.
•Evenings. On the main street in the town centre. •Moderate.
Quieter restaurant/bar run by a friendly Greek/English couple. The menu consists of Greek and 'international' dishes. Live piano and bouzouki *music.*

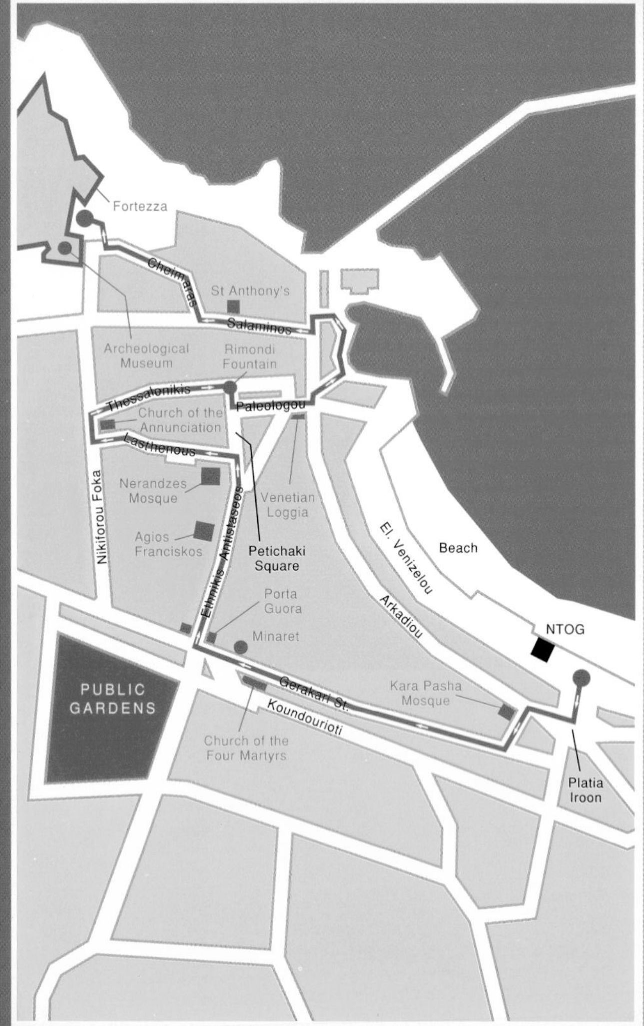

Fortezza
Cheimaras
St Anthony's
Salaminos
Archeological Museum
Rimondi Fountain
Thessalonikis
Paleologou
Church of the Annunciation
Lasthenous
Nerandzes Mosque
Venetian Loggia
Agios Franciskos
Nikiforou Foka
Ethnikis Antistaseos
Petichaki Square
El. Venizelou
Beach
Arkadiou
Porta Guora
Minaret
NTOG
PUBLIC GARDENS
Gerakari St.
Koundourioti
Kara Pasha Mosque
Church of the Four Martyrs
Platia Iroon

Walk

1 hr-1 hr 30 min.

Start at the seafront near the NTOG office (see **Tourist Information**). Cross Iroon Sq and turn into Victor Ougo St., on the corner of which stands the Kara Pasha Mosque (looking rather forlorn in its neglected garden). Just round the corner is one of the the city's several Turkish fountains. Take a right turn into Gerakari St. and keep going until you reach a large, modern square. The Church of the Four Martyrs is on the left, and a graceful minaret can be seen to the right above the rooftops of the surrounding houses. Enter the old city through the Porta Guora, the only surviving part of the original city walls, and continue down Ethnikis Antistaseos St. Agios Franciskos (see **WHAT TO SEE**), with its partially-restored facade, is down a side passage to the left. At the end of the passage stands the imposing gateway of the Turkish school which still functions as a primary school. Continue along Ethnikis Antistaseos St. and, as you enter Petichaki Sq, turn left into Lasthenous St. which leads to the Nerandzes Mosque (see **WHAT TO SEE**). Climb the graceful minaret and enjoy the splendid views over the city. Lasthenous and the surrounding streets are typical of the older quarter where Venetian doorways and arches exist cheek by jowl with wooden Turkish balconies, and modern dwellings stand next to the empty shells of Venetian houses. Turn right into Nikiforou Foka St. at the top of Lasthenous St. and you will come to a quiet little square containing the Venetian church of the Annunciation. Turn right down Thessalonikis St. and follow it into Petichaki Sq where water still flows from the three lions' head faucets of the Rimondi Fountain (see **WHAT TO SEE, A-Z**). Continue down Paleologou St., passing the Venetian Loggia (see **WHAT TO SEE**), and the adjoining Nearchou St. going towards the harbour. You are now in the lively area of the old Venetian port with its numerous restaurants and discos. Turn left at the end of the harbour into Salaminos St., passing the Catholic church of St Anthony on the right. Take a diagonal right turn down Cheimaras St. which leads to the huge Venetian fortress that dominates the town (see **WHAT TO SEE**, **Rethymnon Fortezza**). Little now remains within its massive ramparts, but the views are wonderful. The Archeological Museum (see **WHAT TO SEE**) is now housed in a restored bastion near the entrance.

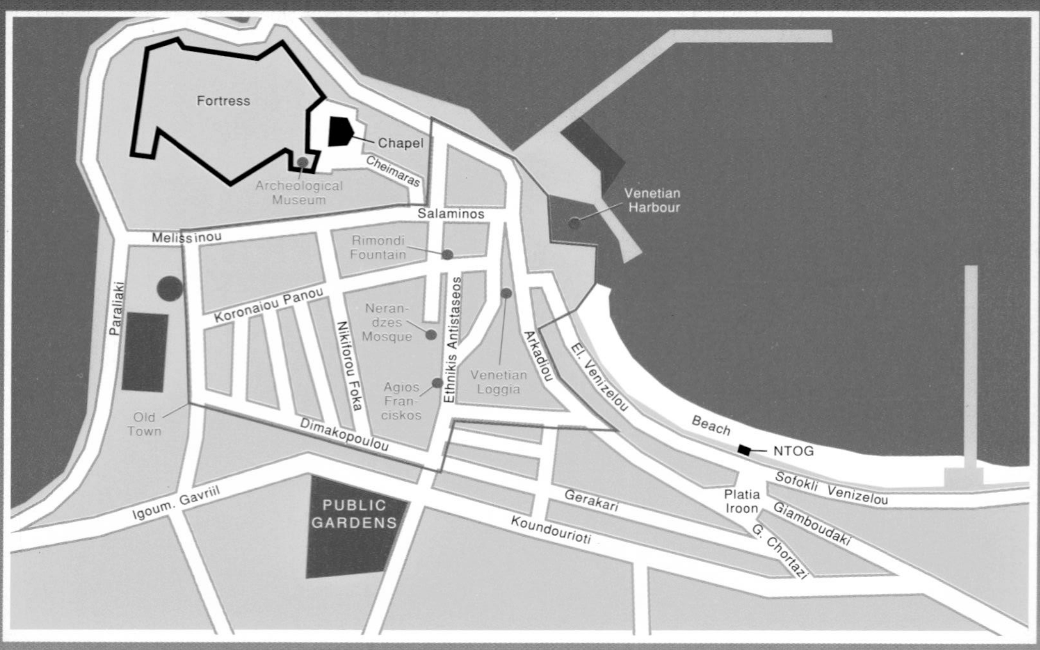
Fortress
Chapel
Cheimaras
Archeological Museum
Salaminos
Venetian Harbour
Melissinou
Rimondi Fountain
Paraliaki
Koronaiou Panou
Neran-dzes Mosque
Ethnikis Antistaseos
Nikiforou Foka
Agios Fran-ciskos
Venetian Loggia
Arkadiou
El. Venizelou
Old Town
Dimakopoulou
Beach
NTOG
Sofokli Venizelou
Platia Iroon
Giamboudaki
G. Chortazi
Gerakari
Koundourioti
Igoum. Gavriil
PUBLIC GARDENS

What to See

ARCHEOLOGICAL MUSEUM

•Check with NTOG for opening times (see **Tourist Information**). At the entrance to the Fortezza.

Local artefacts and finds from the Neolithic period to Venetian times include bronzes, jewellery, sculptures and sarcophagi. See WALK.

FORTEZZA (VENETIAN FORTRESS)

•0900-1630. Overlooking the city at the western end of the seafront.

Impressive ramparts and ruins of the original 16thC stronghold. Good vantage point for views of the town. See WALK, **Rethymnon Fortezza**.

VENETIAN LOGGIA Paleologou St.

•Interior closed. Near the old port.

The town's historic political and commercial meeting place. Impressive 16thC arcaded facade. See WALK.

RIMONDI FOUNTAIN Petichaki Sq.

At the far end of Palelogou St. from the old port.

Early-17thC Venetian fountain decorated with columns and lions' heads. See WALK, **A-Z**.

NERANDZES MOSQUE Lasthenous St.

•1000-1900 Sun.-Fri., 1100-2000 Sat. Off Petichaki Sq.

Mosque with exceptionally striking minaret. Climb its steep spiral stairways for superb views of the town. See WALK.

AGIOS FRANCISKOS Ethnikis Anistaseos St.

•Open for concerts. Near the Nerandzes Mosque.

A remnant of the town's Venetian past. Note the richly-decorated main door. Extensive restorations have transformed the church into an attractive exhibition and concert hall. See WALK.

PUBLIC GARDENS Koundourioti St.

Near the Porta Guora.

Originally an Ottoman graveyard, the public park is now most notable as the site of the annual wine festival in late July (see **Events**).

Accidents and Breakdowns: In the event of an accident, exchange names and insurance details. Only expect police intervention if someone has been injured, in which case you should contact your consulate (see **A-Z**).
If you break down call the ELPA (Hellenic Touring and Automobile Club) which offers a free breakdown service to members of foreign automobile associations (tel: 104). If you are not eligible for this service contact ELPA in Heraklion (tel: 081-289440) or Express Service at Skoula St. 1, Chania (tel: 0821-26059/57177). See **Car Hire, Driving**.

Accommodation: There are six official categories of hotel on Crete, ranging from Luxury through Grades A to E (the last being pretty basic). The quality of the accommodation varies tremendously within each category, but the price is fixed by the government. A double room costs 11,000 Drs per night in a 'Luxury' hotel and 1000 Drs in an 'E'-class hotel. The larger hotels are usually booked up with group reservations, so don't automatically expect to find a room in one of them. If you arrive in Crete without a hotel reservation go to the NTOG office at Chania or Heraklion airports (see **Tourist Information**), or to a travel agent or the Tourist Police (see **Police**).
There are also many rooms to rent in private houses, especially in villages, which are simple, but good value. Self-catering villas and apartments can be very reasonable too, but usually need to be booked in advance. See **Camping**, **Youth Hostels**.

Agia Ekaterini Church, Heraklion: The church was formerly a monastic school and, in the 16th-17thC, a centre of Cretan art, theology, literature and culture. It is now a Museum of Religious Art containing six superb 16thC icons by the great Cretan painter, Damiskinos. See **HERAKLION - WHAT TO SEE.**

Agia Galini: See **HERAKLION - EXCURSION 1.**

Agia Triada Palace: Built around 1600 BC, the palace consists of two perpendicular wings and is believed to have been either a royal retreat from Phaestos (see **HERAKLION - EXCURSION 1, A-Z)** or the residence of a prince. Some of the finest examples of Minoan art have been found here, including frescoes, a painted sarcophagus and three famous vases of black soapstone (the Harvester Vase, the Boxer Vase and the Chieftan Cup) which are now on display in Heraklion's Archeological Museum (see **HERAKLION - WHAT TO SEE, A-Z**). See **HERAKLION - EXCURSION 1.**

Agios Nikolaos: The capital of Lasithi. Pop: 6000. Beautifully situated on the Gulf of Mirabello, the town enjoys a mild, dry climate and a booming tourist industry. The attractive town centre is enhanced by a fresh water lake which is now joined to the open sea by an artificial channel and serves as an inner harbour. A small museum to the north west contains many finds from excavations in the Lasithi province (0845-1500 Wed.-Mon.; 200 Drs). Visitors can enjoy the numerous restaurants, tavernas and cafés around the seafront, lake and harbour areas as well as the rather busy beaches both in and near the town. Boats leave the harbour for other islands such as Karpathos. See **AGIOS NIKOLAOS - BEACHES, EXCURSIONS, NIGHTLIFE, RESTAURANTS, WHAT TO SEE.**

Airports: There are two main airports on Crete:
Heraklion (tel: 081-282025) - 3 km east of the capital. Handles international flights, daily flights to Rhodes, Mykonos and Athens (seven), and air links to other islands. Airport facilities include an information desk, a duty-free shop, a restaurant, a meeting point and car-hire representatives. Olympic Airways runs a bus link to Heraklion (150 Drs) and there is also a cheaper local bus service (50 Drs). The same journey by taxi costs about 250 Drs per person.
Chania - 15 km from Chania town. Mainly handles internal and charter flights. The airport is smaller than Heraklion's and there are fewer facilities. The Olympic Airways bus link to town costs 150 Drs, the local bus costs 50 Drs and taxis cost about 500 Drs per person.
In addition, a very small airport at Sitia (see **AGIOS NIKOLAOS - BEACHES, EXCURSION 1**) operates scheduled flights to Rhodes, via the islands of Kassos and Karpathos, four times a week.

Amnisos: 7 km east of Heraklion. This was the principal port serving Knossos during the Minoan period and excavations have revealed a villa and shrine dating from that time. The famous *Frescoes of the Lilies* (c.1600 BC) found on the site are housed in the Archeological Museum at Heraklion (see **HERAKLION - WHAT TO SEE, A-Z**). The beach here, which has plenty of tavernas and cafés nearby, is one of the capital's closest and can be reached by bus No.1 from the city.

Antiques: It is illegal to take Greek antiques out of the country without prior permission, which involves an enormous amount of paper work, and those found guilty of illegally exporting antiques face prosecution and stiff penalties. It is probably advisable to settle for some of the excellent copies of ancient icons and antique jewellery available on the island, or else try to find old embroidery and costumes in the various flea markets.

Aptera: The ruins of an ancient city, 15 km to the east of Chania, with magnificent views over Soudha Bay. It survived into the early Christian era before being plundered by Arab pirates. A monastery, enclosed by the city walls, marks the centre of the site, which includes a classical Greek temple and theatre, underground arched cisterns and a Byzantine temple. The Turkish fortress of Izzedin, standing on the outskirts, guarded the entrance to Soudha harbour.

Archeological Museum, Chania: Housed in the church of Agios Francisko, once one of Crete's finest churches, the museum displays finds from the excavations at Aptera (see **A-Z**) and Polyrrinia. The range of exhibits dates back to Neolithic times and includes inscribed tablets, Minoan seals and pottery, Greek and Roman glassware, classical sculptures and mosaics. See **CHANIA - WHAT TO SEE**.

Archeological Museum, Heraklion: One of the world's finest archeological museums traces Crete's ancient past up to Roman times and houses some splendid Minoan treasures. The rooms are well laid out in chronological and geographical order. The following exhibits should not be missed:

Room 3 - fine Kamares ceramics (see **HERAKLION - EXCURSION 1**); the Phaestos Disk with its undeciphered hieroglyphics (see **HERAKLION - EXCURSION 1**).

Room 4 - the famous representations of the Snake Goddess from Knossos (see **A-Z**); the sacred Bull's Head vessel of black stone encrusted with rock crystal and mother-of-pearl; a beautifully-made games board; a giant royal sword from Malia Palace (see **A-Z**).

Room 7 - three stone vases and gold jewellery from Agia Triada (see **HERAKLION - EXCURSION 1, A-Z**).

Room 8 - a beautiful rock crystal vase from Zakros Palace (see **A-Z**), found in 300 pieces and painstakingly reconstructed.

Room 13 - a wooden model of the palace of Knossos (see **A-Z**).

Room 14 - reconstructed Minoan frescoes including the *Prince of Lilies* and *La Parisienne* from Knossos (see **A-Z**), and the *Red and White Lilies* from Amnisos (see **A-Z**); a sarcophagus (1400 BC) from Agia Triada (see **HERAKLION - EXCURSION 1**, **A-Z**) dominates the centre of the room. See **HERAKLION - WHAT TO SEE**.

Babysitters: Ask at your hotel reception or speak to you travel representative. The service is likely to cost about 500 Drs per hour. See **Children**.

Banks: See **Money, Opening Times.**

Beaches: There are marvellous beaches with clear water to be found all round the coastline of Crete, but the best and generally the quieter beaches are in the south. Some beaches do, however, suffer from oil pollution and the water is not always clean, especially near the larger towns. Some of the bigger hotels have private beaches and there are also municipal beaches, popular with families, which have showers and changing cabins (and cost upwards of 150 Drs). You can hire canoes, pedal boats and windsurfing boards, or water-ski, at most of the resort beaches. Always be careful of strong currents and undertows. See **BEACHES, Sport**.

Best Buys: As on most of the Greek islands, local crafts are the best buys. These include jewellery, leather goods, pottery, knitwear and embroidery. All are widely available in the numerous arts-and-crafts shops in all the tourist centres, but try shopping around for quality. For example, in the villages you can try bargaining directly with the crafts-people.

Leather work is particularly abundant in the west of Crete, where it is possible to have shoes made to measure, while the whole of the northern coast, and especially Heraklion, is renowned for its local pottery which can be purchased direct from the factory or at small workshops. The island is also well known for its cloth. *Hyfanda* is the type of weaving (see **Crafts**) that is particular to Crete and many designs are available in it - the centres at Kritsa (see **AGIOS NIKOLAOS - WHAT TO SEE, A-Z**) and Anogia (**HERAKLION - EXCURSION 2**) both produce high-quality work.

Woollens are another good buy and hand-knitted pullovers are extremely good value.
Speciality foods include olive oil, feta (goats' milk cheese) and honey which can all be found in the local markets (see **A-Z**).

Bicycle and Motorbike Hire: Available in the larger towns and villages frequented by tourists. Bicycles are ideal for exploring the immediate vicinity and finding quieter beaches, although the ruggedness of the terrain combined with the heat of summer may make the going a bit difficult. Motorbikes are good for longer distances and avoiding the traffic jams in Heraklion and Chania, but strong winds on the northern coast and rocky dirt roads can be hazardous, so take extra care. You will probably find that scooters lack sufficient power for propelling you up some of the steep roads in the interior. Helmets are seldom provided, but try and acquire one for your own safety.
Bicycles - approx. 500 Drs per day.
Scooters - approx. 1000 Drs per day.
Motorbikes - 1300-3500 Drs per day (when you hire by the week you get two days free).
The minimum age for hiring scooters and motorbikes is 18. A licence is required for larger models of motorbike. Make sure that comprehensive insurance is included in the agreement as, unfortunately, there are many accidents each year caused by inexperienced or careless drivers.

Budget: Crete is still relatively inexpensive, although prices continue to rise in proportion to the growing number of tourists coming to the island.

Bread	50 Drs (1 kg).
Butter	80 Drs (250 g).
Eggs	20 Drs (each).
Fruit juice	200 Drs (1 litre).
Wine	500 Drs (1.5 litres).
Hotel breakfast	approx. 350 Drs.
Lunch	approx. 800 Drs.
Dinner	from 2000 Drs.

Buses: Crete has two types of bus service - local buses, used by the islanders for getting to schools and markets, and KTEL for longer journeys and intended for tourist use (usually more modern). Tourist attractions are usually well served by regular services, but buses coming and going from the smaller villages tend to run at inconvenient times for day excursions.

Heraklion bus stations: Terminus A at the port serves the east coast of the island; Terminus B at Porta Chania serves the south west along inland roads; the station near the Venetian harbour serves the west coast; the smallest station at Kiprou Sq, just outside the walls, serves the south-east (mainly Ierapetra).

Chania bus stations: Buses to Rethymnon/Heraklion from El Venizelou Sq. 28; buses to Kissamos/Selina from Kebaidi Sq.; buses to Apokoronos/Sfakia from Nikiforou/Episkopou.

Rethymnon bus station: Buses to Chania/Heraklion from Agnostou Stratioti Sq.

Agios Nikolaos bus stations: Atlandithos Sq for services to Heraklion, Sitia, Ierapetra and villages along the way; the harbour for buses to Elounda.

Sitia bus station: Papanastasiou St. 4.

The termini in the provincial capitals have cafés and toilet facilities (see **Toilets**). See **Transport**.

Cameras and Photography: Films, video cassettes and flashes are all readily available in the provincial capitals and tourist centres, but they are expensive so stock up before coming. You can take photographs in museums (when it is allowed) and at archeological sites for free when using a small portable camera without a flash, but if you use a tripod you will be charged 1500 Drs. There are restrictions on taking photographs near military or naval installations (such as the naval base at Soudha Bay). You cannot hire video equipment on Crete.

Camping: There are fourteen official campsites on Crete, the most popular being those at Paleochora, Agia Galini, Matala, Chersonisos, Heraklion, Malia and Ierapetra. These provide all the usual facilities and are generally clean and well run. Contact any of the NTOG offices (see **Tourist Information**) for a full list of campsites along with their

telephone numbers. The average cost per night is 200 Drs for an adult and 100 Drs for a child. A car and tent costs an extra 340 Drs. Unofficial camping is now theoretically prohibited on the island, though it is still practised, especially in remoter areas. See **Accommodation, Youth Hostels**.

Car Hire: This can be fairly expensive, but is one of the best ways to see the island. In theory you are required to hold an international driving licence, but in practice most agencies will accept a national one that has been valid for at least one year. The minimum age for hiring a car varies from 21 to 25. Local agencies tend to be cheaper than the well-known international firms, but check that they offer comprehensive insurance. The larger firms have the advantage in that they cover the whole island, allowing you to pick up and drop off a car at different places. They will also provide a replacement in the case of theft or breakdown. However, you will have to leave an extremely large deposit unless you pay by credit card. Try negotiating for a lower rate out of season. See **Accidents and Breakdowns, Driving**.

Caves: There are numerous caves on Crete, because of its limestone formation, which are all linked in some way to the life and history of the islanders. Some, such as those at Matala, have been used as shelters while others, for example at Amnisos, were ancient centres of worship, and still more were places of refuge from the Turks, for instance the ones at Milatos and Melidoni. Around 300 have been excavated so far and have yielded a wealth of archeological remains. If you wish to visit any of the caves, check beforehand that they are not under excavation as this may mean that they have been fenced off at the entrance. If, however, the cave you want to visit is open, then go properly equipped with torches, warm clothing and good footwear. See **Diktaean Cave, Eileithia Cave, Idaian Cave, Melidoni Cave, Sendoni Cave.**

Ceremonies: The traditional marriage ceremony is one of the most colourful ceremonies in Crete. In former days the whole village helped the young couple begin their life together by building their house, cutting the wood to cook their first meal and warm them through their first winter, and baking and decorating the *koularia* (wedding cakes). On the day of the wedding, baskets of provisions are taken as gifts to the new house, and at midday the dowry is taken to the bridegroom's house in a procession led by a lyre player. After the ceremony, which includes the symbolic exchange of crowns, the villagers pin bank notes to the bride's dress and the parents hang gold coins round her neck. Two knives placed at the entrance to the new house are intended to chase away evil spirits, and the bride throws in a few grains of grenadine to ensure future happiness. You can still see traditional weddings at the village of Anogia (see **HERAKLION - EXCURSION 2**) and the ceremony is laid on for tourists in late August at Kritsa (see **AGIOS NIKOLAOS - WHAT TO SEE, A-Z**). See **Customs**.

Chania: The capital of the province of Chania and the former capital of the island. Pop: 40,000. Chania is a beautiful town of great historical interest - it was built on the ruins of the ancient city of Kydonia. During the Second World War it suffered heavy bombardment which destroyed virtually all of the town apart from the area around the old port where you can still see examples of Venetian and Turkish architecture in the quarters known as Splanzia and Kastelli. The old town also has a large number of leather shops selling bags, sandals and boots (see **Best Buys**). The new town boasts a splendid municipal market building, constructed in the form of a cross, which is supposedly modelled on a market at Marseilles (see **Markets**). The Historical Museum and Archives, to the south east of the town, contains an interesting collection of Turkish and Venetian manuscripts, and the Municipal Gardens has a tiny zoo, a children's playground, a café and an auditorium. This last is used as an open-air cinema and venue for folk displays and cultural performances - contact the NTOG office for details (see **Tourist Information**). See **CHANIA - BEACHES, EXCURSION, NIGHTLIFE, RESTAURANTS, WHAT TO SEE.**

Chemists: The sign for a chemist's is a green or red cross on a white background. Most chemists keep normal opening hours (see **Opening Times**), but they also operate a rota system so that at least one shop is open outside normal hours. Details are displayed in the window of every chemist.

Chersonisos: The small port of Limin Chersonisos, to give it its full and proper title, lies 29 km to the east of Heraklion and has become one of the largest tourist centres on Crete, with hotels, restaurants and beaches catering for all tastes. However, some of the port's charm remains in spite of the recent influx of visitors. The port flourished during the Roman and Byzantine periods and you can see submerged Roman ruins along the shoreline. The village of Chersonisos lies 2 km inland from the port. See **HERAKLION - BEACHES**.

Children: The Cretan people adore children and make them welcome in most establishments, even late at night. Most public gardens in the provincial capitals provide swings and slides, and there is often a funfair just outside the one in Heraklion. Most of the larger hotels also provide amenities to keep children amused. If your child gets lost contact the Tourist Police (see **Emergency Numbers**, **Police**).
See **Babysitters**.

Cigarettes: Most international brands of cigarette are readily available on Crete, but foreign cigarettes, costing between 200-250 Drs, are considerably more expensive than Greek brands. Cigarettes are sold at kiosks called *periptero*.

Climate: Spring (average temperature 15°C-21°C) and autumn (18°C-21°C) are possibly the best times to visit Crete, as the weather is not too hot and the sea is warm enough to swim in. The island is at its most verdant and colourful in spring. The hottest months are July and August (25°C-26°C), but the summer temperatures are mitigated by the prevailing *meltemi,* a seasonal wind blowing from the north. Winters are mild and often quite wet.

Complaints: Crete relies heavily on tourism, so you are unlikely to be overcharged. However, if you do feel that you have been unfairly treated, ask to see the owner or manager of the premises. If you are still not satisfied, then you can report the establishment to the Tourist Police (see **Police**), but you will find that just threatening this course of action is usually sufficient.

Consulates:
UK - Papalexandrou St. 16, Heraklion, Crete, tel: 081-224012.
Republic of Ireland - Vass. Constantinou 7, Athens, tel: 721-2951.
USA - Vas. Sofias Av 91, Athens, tel: 721-2951.
Canada - Grennadiou 4, Athens, tel: 723-9511.
Australia - Dimitriou Soutso 37, Athens, tel: 644-7303.
New Zealand - Ari Tsoha 15-17, Athens, tel: 641-0311.

Conversion Charts:

TEMPERATURE

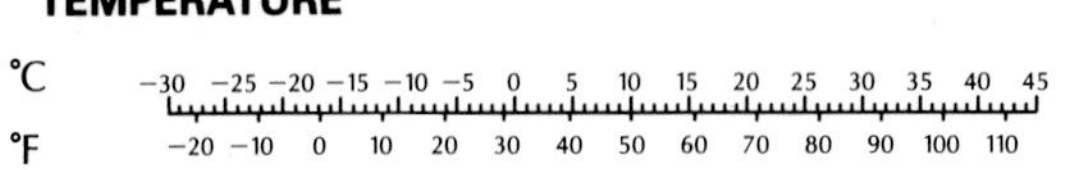

DISTANCE

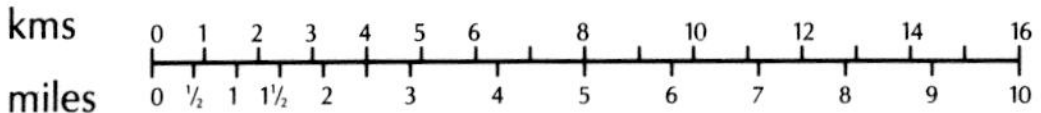

WEIGHT

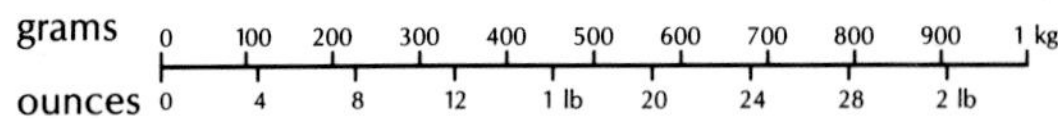

Crafts: Weaving is a major form of Cretan popular art involving techniques which are handed down from mother to daughter, with each weaver adding her own personal touch to the age-old designs. All the materials used - wool, cotton, linen, and silk and vegetable dyes - are home-produced. Traditionally, when Cretan men choose a bride, her skill in weaving is regarded as of the upmost importance. See HERAKLION - EXCURSION 2, **Best Buys, Kritsa**.

Credit Cards: See **Money**.

Crime and Theft: The Cretan people are renowned for being honest and trustworthy, and theft on Crete is rare (another tourist is more likely to rob you than a Cretan). Nevertheless take care of your property and leave valuables in the hotel safe. If you are the victim of a theft, contact the police (see **A-Z**) and, if necessary, your own consulate (see **A-Z**). Remember to keep a copy of the police report for any insurance claim you may make (see **Insurance**). If you are arrested for any reason, get in touch with your consulate immediately - they are obliged to find you an English-speaking lawyer. See **Emergency Numbers**.

Currency: The drachma is the national monetary unit of Greece (abbreviated as Drs). Coins in circulation are worth 1, 2, 5, 10, 20 and 50 Drs. Notes are in denominations of 50, 100, 500, 1000 and 5000 Drs. See **Money**, **Telephones and Telegrams**.

Customs:

Duty Paid Into:	Cigarettes (or)	Cigars (or)	Tobacco	Spirits	Wine
E.E.C.	300	75	400 g	1.5 *l*	5 *l*
U.K.	300	75	400 g	1.5 *l*	5 *l*

Customs, Cretan: One of the most pleasant Cretan customs, the *volta,* is a pastime shared by the inhabitants of all the warm, southern-European countries. This early-evening, pre-dinner promenade is very much a social institution, usually taking place along the harbour fronts of the seaside towns and along the roads of the inland villages. In the capital, head for Elefterias Square if you want to join the crowd.
Like all Greeks, the Cretans are a very hospitable people. Don't be offended by their curiosity which should be taken as a sign of politeness and genuine interest. In Cretan homes it is customary for the mis-

tress of the house to ply a visitor with food and refreshments without taking any herself - accept any hospitality proffered to you gracefully. Never make a gesture with the palm of your hand facing outwards as this is considered grossly insulting. Lastly, if you are told that something will be ready tomorrow (*avrio*) then it may not necessarily mean the next day, so be prepared to wait. See **Ceremonies**, **Language**.

Dia Island: A small rocky islet, 12 km north east of Heraklion, which is one of three sanctuaries for the long-horned wild goats known as *kri-kri*. The little church of Analipsi hosts a saint's day feast (see **Festivities**) in June and there is a taverna which opens up here during the summer when there are regular boat services to the island.

Diktaean Cave: The mythical birthplace of Zeus (see **Myths and Legends**) situated above the Lasithi Plateau near Psychro. Excavations began here in the late 19thC and have yielded rich finds. There is evidence that the cave was used as a centre of cult worship in the Minoan period. The interior has impressive stalactites and stalagmites. Visitors to the cave are recommended to take suitable, non-slip footwear and a torch. See AGIOS NIKOLAOS - EXCURSION 2, **Caves**.

Disabled: Crete has few facilities for disabled people. In addition, the general lack of organization and the mountainous nature of the landscape can make things very difficult for the handicapped. Notify hotels in advance if you have any special requirements, and remember to read the small print on insurance documents (see **Insurance**). It also may not be possible to obtain certain medicines, so be sure to stock up at home before you go on holiday. See **Health**.

Drinks: Crete boasts a variety of different wines, ranging from the well-known Vin Castel to the red, robust wines of the Sitia region and the excellent wines of Archanes and Peza. The ones you are most likely to encounter on Cretan supermarket shelves are Minos, Demestica, Gortys, Olympia and Lato. Of course, the distinctive *retsina*, a resinated wine which is best drunk cold and is a good accompaniment to many meals (something of an acquired taste), is available all over Greece. *Ouzo*, the other national drink, is the most common aperitif. This aniseed spirit is served with water and ice. Metaxa is a Greek brandy that is sweeter and often rougher than its French counterpart, although it comes in a range (one to seven stars) of qualities. Beer is extremely popular on the island. Both of the local brands, Fix and Hellas, are widely available, as are imported lagers. *Raki* (*tzikoudia*), an exceptionally strong spirit, is somewhat of a Cretan speciality. Served in little glasses, usually as an aperitif, it should be swallowed in one gulp! Greek coffee comes in very small cups, is extremely strong and black and is served with a glass of water. Order it *glikos* if you want it very sweet, *metrios* for medium sweet and *sketos* for plain. If you don't want it at all ask for a Nescafé. You can drink the tap water, but most people prefer to buy bottled water which is available nearly everywhere.

Driving: You must have an EC or international driving licence and third-party insurance to drive in Greece. Green Card insurance is also recommended. Drive on the right-hand side and give way to traffic coming from the right. Seat belts are now compulsory.
The one main road running along the north coast of the island from Chania to Sitia is in very good condition and there is a provincial network of secondary roads which are mostly surfaced, but are less well

maintained and are pitted by occasional potholes. The mountain roads are narrow with incredibly sharp bends. Be sure to sound your horn as you approach bends as Cretan driving tends to be fast and erratic and many people, and stray animals, walk on the roads. Don't embark on any journeys by car without a detailed map as many roads are not well signposted and you could easily lose your way. In Heraklion, cars with even registration numbers can only be used on even-numbered dates and cars with odd numbers can only be used on odd dates, but this does not apply to foreign or rented cars. Observe the local speed limits and parking regulations, and don't drink and drive as this is an offence. Although there are numerous petrol stations around the island there are fewer in the remoter regions and in the south, so keep a full tank. You can buy lead-free petrol at the Shell stations on Soudhas Av, Chania, and at Mafsotou St. 13 and Ikarou Av 15, Heraklion. See **Car Hire**.

Drugs: All drugs are illegal and there are severe penalties for offenders, ranging from prison sentences of up to one year for possession of even small amounts of hashish, to life imprisonment and hefty fines for anyone suspected of dealing in drugs.

Eating Out: There are restaurants catering for every taste in all the larger towns and tourist resorts, but the smaller villages usually only possess tavernas, which are usually more informal, cheaper, family-run establishments where you will often be invited into the kitchen to choose what you want to eat. For authentic Greek cooking go to a taverna frequented by local people, even if the decor is not inspiring (spontaneous dancing may start later on in the evening). Desserts are not usually served in tavernas (although this is changing to cater for foreign tastes) and it is customary to go to a pastry shop after a meal. Before the meal it is traditional to go for an appetizer at an *ouzerie* where you will be served with *ouzo* and snacks known as *mezedes*. There is a tradition of serving food at lukewarm temperatures, and sometimes several courses appear at once. Specify if you want things done differently. The menu in restaurants and tavernas, when there is one, always has two sets of prices (with and without service charges). You pay the more expensive of the two. See RESTAURANTS, **Food**.

Eileithia Cave: This cave, 1 km from Amnisos, was consecrated to Ilithya, the goddess of childbirth, and was an important shrine of cult worship from Neolithic to Roman times. You can reach it on bus No. 1 from Heraklion. See **Caves**.

Electricity: 220 volts. Small two-pin plugs are used and adaptors are available in Greece and the UK.

Elyros: One of two ancient sites near the town of Sougia, 67 km south west of Chania. This Doric settlement possesses the ruins of a theatre, an aqueduct and a church. To get to it take the Sougia bus from Kydonias St., Chania and then be prepared for a 1 hr walk. There is no entrance fee. See **Lissos**.

Emergency Numbers:

Police	100.
Ambulance	166.
Tourist Police	171.

See **Children**, **Crime and Theft**, **Health**, **Police**.

Evans, Sir Arthur John (1851-1941): The English archeologist and former curator of the Ashmolean Museum responsible for the excavations at Knossos (see **A-Z**) in the first half of this century. This resulted in his discovery of a pre-Phoenician script and a separate and distinct Bronze Age civilization he called Minoan. One of his most famous publications was entitled *The Palace of Minos at Knossos.*

Events:
6 January (Epiphany) - Blessing of the Water, a ceremony (intended to chase away the spirits of the 12 days of Christmas) in which a cross is blessed then thrown into the water. Young men and boys dive in to retrieve it and the winner receives a cash prize.
Fortnight before Lent - The Carnival, costumed processions and festivities best enjoyed in Heraklion and Rethymnon; *last Monday before Lent* - Clean Monday, a day to fly kites and take picnics before the period of abstinence begins.
Easter weekend (Greek Orthodox Calendar) - ceremonies, processions, church services, the lighting of candles, fireworks, celebrations and feasting.

25 March - Independence Day, processions and general celebrations to commemorate the revolt against the Turks in 1821.
1 May - May Day or Spring Festival, a national holiday with dancing and feasting; *20-27* - Anniversary of the Battle of Crete (Second World War), dancing, sports events and ceremonies in Chania and a different village each year.
24 June - Feast of St John the Baptist and Summer Solstice, bonfires all over the island; *late June* - Naval or Marine Week, fireworks, naval displays and sea sports, especially at Soudha.
15-31 July - Rethymnon Wine Festival, folk dancing and the sampling of wines.
July-August - Heraklion Festival, cultural events include drama, dance, classical music, jazz and films.
15 August - Assumption of the Virgin Mary, dancing, fireworks, sports and craft displays, pilgrimage to the island of Tinos, feasts in many villages and at many monasteries, but chiefly celebrated in Mokhos (near Malia) and Neapoli; *31 August* - Consecration of the Virgin, festivals and dancing at Psychro village on the Lasithi Plateau (see **AGIOS NIKOLAOS - EXCURSION 2**).
28 October - Ochi ('No') Day, national holiday commemorating Greece's rejection of Mussolini's ultimatum of 1940.
7-9 November - Moni Arkadi Explosion, large celebration commemorating those who died in the 1886 explosion at Moni Arkadi (see **A-Z**).
See **Festivities, Public Holidays**.

Ferries: Chania and Heraklion are the main departure points for Pireas (the port of Athens), the Peloponnese and the Cyclades, though some lines covering these destinations also leave from Agios Nikolaos and Sitia (tel: 0843-22310).
Chania's port is at Soudha, 7 km west of the town. Local buses leave from the market place (see **CHANIA - WHAT TO SEE**) every 15 min (approx.). Most of the ferries arrive in the morning and leave in the evening. For information on those running directly to and from Pireas, tel: 0821-23636, or via the Peloponnese, tel: Pireas 01-4172657. The journey takes 11 hr and single tickets cost 1800-4200 Drs per person and 4500 Drs per car.

AVRA

Heraklion's port has ferry services to Pireas (tel: 081-226481; takes 12 hr; tickets 2000-4500 Drs), Mykonos (via Santorini, Ios, Naxos and Paros), Cyprus and Egypt. Port facilities include a bar, a restaurant, a post office, telephones, toilets, showers and an information service.
Rethymnon Port is a picturesque little port with only a few services. Tel: 081-226697 for information.
Agios Nikolaos' port is served by two lines running to the Dodecanese and the Cyclades, including the islands of Kassos, Karpathos, Chalki, Rhodes, Simi, Tilos, Nissiros, Kos, Kalymnos, Astipalea, Amorgos, Anafi, Santorini, Milos and Paros. Tel: 0841-22312 for information.

Festivities: The main festivities on the island occur on the feast days of the local patron saints. The *panegyria,* as it is called, really begins in each village on the eve of the feast day, when everyone from the surrounding countryside gathers to spend the night singing and dancing. The celebrations then begin all over again after Mass the following day. Traditionally, visitors who come to experience the festivities are made welcome guests of the village and are offered hospitality in every house (see **Customs**). Needless to say, with growing numbers of tourists flocking to the villages to see the celebrations, it is not practicable for the local people to honour this tradition today, although you may still get a taste of it in remoter villages during the low season. See **Ceremonies**, **Events**.

Fodele: A picturesque village in attractive countryside 22 km east of Heraklion. Once considered to be the birthplace of El Greco (see **A-Z**), there are various memorials honouring him here. You can reach the village by bus from Heraklion's Porta Chania.

Folk Dancing: Typical Cretan folk dancing takes the form of a chain, with the dancers holding each other by the hand or shoulder. Unlike many Greek dances, everyone dances, not just the leaders of the chain. All the dances are accompanied by at least one musician and singing. The following dances are the most common:
Kastrinos - A slow rhythmic dance with small steps, which comes from Heraklion.

Pendozalis - A fast, spirited dance popular all over Crete, which was made famous in the film *Zorba the Greek*.
Sousta - An erotic, improvised dance for two, originating in Rethymnon, which demands a certain degree of grace, suppleness and imagination.
Syrtos - Another circle dance in which the leader sometimes performs spectacular routines.

Folk Music: The origins of Cretan music would appear be rooted in early Minoan culture.
Cretan songs are characterized by a rich expressiveness, yet they are also tender. Although a limited range of notes is used, the music is normally lively and the melody forceful. The two basic types of folk song are *mandinades*, a living form reflecting the traditional character of the Cretan people and tending to deal with universal subjects such as love and death, and *rizitika*, songs of the White Mountains with somewhat sentimental heroic or patriotic themes which constitute a fairly sophisticated form of Cretan popular poetry (usually accompanied by the *bouzouki*).
The main musical instrument in Crete is the lyre (*lyra*) which is derived from the smaller *lyriki*. Other traditional instruments include the *laouto* (a type of mandolin), the *askomantoura* (resembling bagpipes), and the *habioli* or shepherd's flute. The *bouzouki*, brought from the Orient by refugees in the 1920s, is popular all over Greece. It was banned for a while by the government, but is now experiencing a revival among modern Greek composers.

Food: Typical Greek dishes include:
Moussaka - aubergines, minced meat, potatoes and béchamel sauce.
Pastitsio - macaroni, minced meat and béchamel sauce.
Dolmades - stuffed vine leaves.
Souvlaki - pieces of meat cooked on a skewer, served with spices and tomatoes, or in pitta bread with salad. The Greek equivalent of a kebab.
Keftedhes - spicy meatballs.
Taramosalata - salad dip of fish roe mixed with cream, olive oil and spices.

Tzatziki - cucumber, yoghurt and garlic salad dip.
Greek salad - feta cheese (goats' milk cheese), tomatoes, lettuce and olives.
Mezedes - a variety of small dishes served with an aperitif (traditionally an *ouzo* - see **Drinks**) or as a starter.
Hummus - pureed chick peas, *tahini* (sesame cream), lemon juice, garlic and olive oil served as a starter.
Local specialities:
Mizithra - unsalted cream cheese used in pies.
Yoghurt - often served with honey for breakfast.
Madares - meat stew with cheese and potatoes.
Kallitsounia - cheese and cinnamon pie.
Barbounia - red mullet served whole (tends to be expensive).
Calamaria - rings of squid fried in batter.
See **RESTAURANTS**, **Eating Out**.

Frangokastello: The fortress of Frangokastello to the east of Chora Sfakion (see **Sfakia**) was built in 1371 as a defence against pirates as well as to maintain order among the local inhabitants. In 1828 Greek rebels occupied the fortress and were subsequently massacred by Turkish invaders. Under certain climatic conditions atmospheric shapes occur which, it is claimed, represent the ghosts of their defeated army. The castle is now largely a ruin, but the beach (see **CHANIA - BEACHES**) is one of the most beautiful on the island.

Gaidhouronisi (Hrisi) Islet: There are one-day excursions by fishing boat (takes 1 hr) from Ierapetra to this tiny (1 km-long) deserted island with its beautiful sandy beaches.

Gavdos Island: A large island, 50 km off Paleochora on the south coast (boats run from there and Chora Sfakion - see **Sfakia)**, with a modern-day population of less than 100. Although it is a barren and inhospitable place, the island does possess magnificent beaches. There is a port at Karabo, an inland capital called Kastri, and two other small settlements at Vatsiana (south of Kastri) and Ambelos (to the north), both of which have marvellous beaches. There is no mains electricity, limited supplies of fresh water and only a few vehicles on the island, so be prepared to walk. Food supplies are also limited as the island depends, to a large extent, on imported goods.

Gortys: This site (46 km south west of Heraklion), now occupied by the remains of a large Greco-Roman city, was inhabited as early as Minoan times, but flourished under Dorian rule. The most fascinating discovery from the site is a series of stone tablets dating from the 5thC BC inscribed with the Law Code of Gortyn. This describes, in Dorian-Greek dialect (running from left to right, then right to left, and so on), the penalties for certain crimes as well as legislates on civil matters.

After the period of Dorian rule Gortys continued to prosper under the Romans and most of the remains are from that era, including an odeon (part of which was built with Law Code stones), a sanctuary and an amphitheatre. You can also see the remains of a large 7thC church, the Basilica of Agios Titus (see **Saint Titus**). The Byzantine city of Gortys was finally destroyed by Arab raiders in AD 824 after already suffering the effects of catastrophic earthquakes. See **HERAKLION - EXCURSION 1.**

Gournia: This extremely well-preserved Minoan town, 19 km south east of Agios Nikalaos, reached the peak of its prosperity during the middle-Minoan period. Outstanding among the many remaining buildings are the small Palace of the Overlord and the public courtyard or marketplace. The wide variety of finds, now housed in the Archeological Museum of Heraklion (see **HERAKLION - WHAT TO SEE, A-Z**), supports the theory that Gournia was once a wealthy and important centre. See **AGIOS NIKOLAOS - WHAT TO SEE.**

Greco, El (1541-1614): The great Greek painter Domenikos Theotokopoulos was born on Crete, possibly in the town of Fodele (see **A-Z**), but more likely in Heraklion (See **A-Z**). He left the island as a young man and acquired his artistic reputation after working and studying in Italy and Spain, but was in the habit of appending *Kres,* or Cretan, to his name.

Hairdressers: There are modern salons in the provincial capitals, the main tourist centres and many of the larger hotels. These tend to be much cheaper than their counterparts in the rest of Europe. Women should expect to pay 800-1200 Drs for having their hair cut and up to 3000 Drs for a perm. Men will have to pay about 200 Drs for a shave and anything up to 1000 Drs for a haircut. See **Tipping**.

Health: Before leaving the UK you should obtain form E 111 from the Department of Social Security which entitles you to free medical treatment in Greece (present it to any State doctor you consult, who will arrange for you to be exempted from payment). However, standards of health care in Greece are less than adequate and it is also advisable to

private health insurance policy to cover private treatment and the cost of repatriation in case of serious illness (see **Insurance**). The following are hospitals with outpatient departments:
General State Hospital, Dragoumi St., Chania, tel: 27231.
Rethymnon Hospital, Hiliakaki St., Rethymnon, tel: 29271.
Venizelou Hospital (near Knossos), Heraklion, tel: 231932.
For treatment in Agios Nikolaos, tel: 22369; in Sitia, tel: 22231.
If you have any trouble finding an English-speaking doctor then contact the NTOG office (see **Tourist Information**) which keeps a list. There are no vaccination requirements unless you are coming from a country where there has been an epidemic. See **Disabled.**

Heraklion: The commercial and political capital of Crete and the fifth- largest city in Greece. Pop: 100,000 plus.
The old city of Heraklion and its chief tourist attractions (the harbour, museums, churches and monuments) lie within the 5 km-long 15thC Venetian walls with their four gates and seven bastions. Much of the city's commercial activity occurs in the modern part of town outwith the old walls, while the port supports a constant sea traffic with the mainland and other islands (see **Ferries**). An airport just outside the

capital handles both international and inter-island flights (see **Airports**). Heraklion also boasts a bustling nightlife with a variety of restaurants and discos. See **BEACHES, EXCURSIONS, NIGHTLIFE, RESTAURANTS, WHAT TO SEE.**

Historical and Ethnographical Museum, Heraklion: The museum houses a wide variety of displays tracing the history and culture of the island from the period when Knossos flourished as its capital up to the present day, including the Byzantine, Venetian and Turkish eras. Exhibits include sculptures, inscribed tablets, religious objects, carvings, icons, and flags and arms dating from the struggle for liberation. There is also a vaulted chapel decorated with 15thC frescoes, the reconstructed study of the writer, Nikos Kazantzakis (see **A-Z**) and the replicated interior of a traditional Cretan home. - plus some fine examples of Cretan handiwork (see **Crafts**). See **HERAKLION - WHAT TO SEE.**

Idaian Cave: Another cave associated with Zeus (see **Myths and Legends**). Situated in the Psiloritis Mountains, it has proved to be a rich source of archeological finds which have provided evidence that the cave was once used as a shrine or centre of worship. It consists of a

0
1
2
3
4
5

long, winding passage leading to various inner chambers. Excavations are still under way and access to the interior is currently restricted. See HERAKLION - EXCURSION 2, **Caves**.

Ierapetra: The largest town in the province of Lasithi. Pop: 9000. Situated 36 km from Agios Nikolaos, Ierapetra is now a largely modern development, although the remains of a Roman theatre can still be seen at the entrance to the town on the Viannos road, a Venetian fortress overlooks the harbour and there is a mosque dating from the Turkish occupation. The town's numerous hotels, restaurants and discos testify to its role as a major tourist resort, and it is possible to swim here even in winter due to the warm African winds. See **AGIOS NIKOLAOS - BEACHES, EXCURSION 1**.

Insurance: You should take out travel insurance covering you against theft and loss of property and money, as well as medical expenses, for the duration of your stay. Your travel agent should be able to recommend a suitable policy. See also **Crime and Theft**, **Driving**, **Health**.

Kamares Cave: See **HERAKLION - EXCURSION 1**, **Caves**.

Kazantzakis, Nikos (1883-1957): One of Greece's greatest writers was born in Heraklion. As a boy he was greatly influenced by the 1897 revolution and later went to study in France. A profound socialist, his best known works include *Freedom or Death*, *Alexis Zorbas* and *Christ Recrucified.* Another of his books, *The Last Temptation,* has been made into a film by Scorsese which has caused much controversy - but this would be nothing new for Kazantzakis who was constantly at loggerheads with the church because of his religious opinions (he was eventually excommunicated, died in exile and was refused a Catholic burial). He was buried in Heraklion where you can visit his tomb, with its famous inscription (see **HERAKLION - WHAT TO SEE**), and a room devoted to him in the city's Historical and Ethnographical Museum (see **HERAKLION - WHAT TO SEE**, **A-Z**).

Knossos: The reconstructed palace at Knossos, the capital of the

Minoan kingdom, is the most famous and impressive archeological site on Crete. According to legend, King Minos created the labyrinth here to hide the Minotaur (see **Myths and Legends**). The frescoed palace was erected in 1400 BC and discovered by Arthur Evans (see **A-Z**) in 1880. He devoted 43 years of his life to excavating it and his reconstruction has always aroused controversy since much of it was based on speculation. The maze of rooms is built round a central courtyard, and there is a sophisticated water and drainage system. The main features include the central court, the Queen's chambers, the throne room and the grand staircase, an excellent piece of design allowing light into the lower storeys of the palace. To get the most out of a visit to Knossos, splash out and buy one of the detailed, but rather expensive, guidebooks available in shops in the capital. It is open 0800-1900, the entrance fee is 500 Drs and you can get there on bus No. 2 from Heraklion city centre (leaves every 20 min). Finds from the site are

exhibited in Heraklion's Archeological Museum (see **HERAKLION - WHAT TO SEE, A-Z**).

Kournas Lake: Crete's only freshwater lake lies 10 km south west of Georgioupolis and can be reached either by car, or by bus to Georgioupolis and then taxi. It offers a pleasant contrast to the more dramatic scenery of the rest of the island and is home to many birds and animals, including birds of prey.

Kourtaliotis Gorge: This wild, narrow, 2000 m-long gorge, with its several caves and springs, is situated 22 km south of Rethymnon and starts at the village of Koxares. You can reach it by taking the Plakias bus and getting off at the stop for Kourtaliotis. Steps down from the road lead to the entrance..See **RETHYMNON - EXCURSION**.

Kritsa: This picturesque village, 11 km from Agios Nikolaos, is the largest of the island's villages and is famous for weaving (see **Best Buys**, **Crafts**), delicious locally-produced honey and magnificent views of the valley (especially from the terraces of its cafés). The people of Kritsa still wear traditional costumes. Visit the Byzantine church of Panagia Kera (1 km outside the village) which has three naves and is decorated throughout with well-preserved 14th-15thC frescoes. See **AGIOS NIKOLAOS - WHAT TO SEE**, **Ceremonies**.

Language: Many casual visitors to Greece are put off any attempt to master the Greek language by the unfamiliar alphabet and the importance of pronouncing words with the proper stress. More problems arise from the transliteration of Greek words into English (especially in place names) as it is possible to be confronted with several variations. For example, Heraklion can also be spelt as Iraklion and Herakleion; Chania may appear as Khania or Hania; and Agios Nikolaos might be written as Ayios Nikolaos. However, it is worthwhile trying to learn a few basic phrases as this will be appreciated by the local inhabitants. See **Customs, Cretan**.

Lasithi Plateau: The fertile plain of Lasithi, over 800 m high and

approximately 10 km by 6 km wide, is covered by a glorious patchwork of cultivated fields (irrigated by numerous windmills) and is surrounded by the impressive Dikti Mountains (home of the famous Diktaean Cave - see **A-Z**). Villages situated around the rim of the plateau are connected by a circular road. See **AGIOS NIKOLAOS - EXCURSION 2**.

Laundries: Launderettes are very rare on Crete and any available laundry services tend to be extremely expensive. Some of the hotels may offer the service to their guests, otherwise you may as well do your own washing - it will dry very quickly in the warm climate.

Leben: An ancient hilltop sanctuary and spa, dating from the 3rdC BC, once well known for its therapeutic spring waters. Situated just to the east of the seaside village of Lendas, 80 km south west of Heraklion, the site can be reached twice daily by bus from the capital.

Lissos: One of two ancient sites near the town of Sougia, 67 km south west of Chania. This settlement has the ruins of a temple and cliff carvings. To get to it take the Sougia bus from Kydonias St., Chania and then be prepared for a 1 hr walk. There is no entrance fee. See **Elyros.**

Lost Property: If you lose anything, contact the local Tourist Police (see **Police**) and the chances are you will recover it.

Malia Palace: 4 km from Malia (see **HERAKLION - BEACHES**) and attractively situated overlooking the sea, the palace is less impressive than either Knossos or Phaestos, but has a great many remains dating from 1700-1450 BC, including the ruins of courtyards, royal apartments, halls, corridors, storage areas, pillars, loggia, staircases, altars and a sacrificial pit. The palace was destroyed in 1700 BC and was reconstructed at a later date. The entrance fee to the site is 200 Drs and you can get there by bus from Heraklion harbour.

Markets: Crete has many lively, colourful markets where you can find a variety of local products ranging from food and crafts, to cheap household goods and clothes. The food market in Chania is a dominant feature of the town (see **CHANIA - WHAT TO SEE, Chania**). You can buy the medicinal plant called *dictamo* there, which is used to make a herbal tea and is also rumoured to be an aphrodisiac. Rethymnon has a picturesque market in the centre of town, which offers both foodstuffs and crafts for sale. The market in 1866 St. in Heraklion (near Venizelou Sq) sells oil, honey, plants, wine, fruit and cheeses, as well as crafts and antiques. See **Best Buys**.

Melidoni Cave: This stalactite cave, 25 km east of Rethymnon and 4 km north east of Perama, can be reached either by car or taxi or by a 1-2 hr walk from the village. It is a memorial to over 300 villagers who sheltered here in 1824 from the Turkish forces and were asphyxiated by fires lit at the cave entrance to smoke them out. See **Caves.**

Mohlos Island: There are boat excursions from Agios Nikolaos to this tiny island in the Gulf of Mirabello. It is an ideal place for bathing and there are Minoan tombs and submerged ruins as well as tavernas. See **AGIOS NIKOLAOS - EXCURSION 1**.

Monasteries: There were 376 monasteries (*moni*) and nearly 10,000 monks on Crete during Venetian times. Under both Venetian and Turkish rule, the monasteries enjoyed special concessions and so became places of refuge for many Cretans. They also flourished as intellectual and artistic centres, allowing the development of the famous Cretan School which produced artists such as El Greco (see **A-Z**) and Damaskinos. During the Turkish occupation the monasteries were ideal bases for insurrection, being enclosed by walls with towers, furnished with back exits and situated in beautiful, serene spots that also provided their inhabitants with natural defences.

Money: The main branches of the top banks represented on Crete, the National Bank of Greece, the Ionian Bank and the Commercial Bank, are to be found along 25 Avgoustou St. in Heraklion, with smaller branches in the provincial capitals and the larger villages and tourist resorts (where you should be prepared for long queues).

Traveller's cheques can be cashed in banks, *bureaux de change* and at post offices (see **A-Z**). Some of the larger shops will accept them as well as the more common currencies, such as pounds sterling, dollars, francs and deutschmarks, but offer a lower rate of exchange. Check what this is before you enter into a transaction. Hotels also provide round-the-clock exchange facilities, but again check the rate and their charges before you change money or cash traveller's cheques. Credit cards and traveller's cheques are accepted by many of the larger, more expensive restaurants, shops, hotels and car-hire firms. Remember to take your passport when changing money and cheques. See **Car Hire**, **Crime and Theft**, **Currency**, **Opening Times**, **Passports and Customs**.

Moni Agia Triada: A renowned early-17thC monastery, 16.5 km north east of Chania, which was founded by the converted Venetian family of Tzangarola (the Venetian influence is apparent in its architecture). The main attractions include the courtyard and some interesting icons. You can reach the monastery by bus from Chania.

Moni Angarathos: A 16thC monastery, 24 km south of Heraklion,

which was a seat of great learning during the Cretan renaissance. It also played an important role in the Turkish-Venetian war of the 17thC. The courtyards are particularly attractive.

Moni Arkadi: 16thC monastery which became famous as a symbol of Cretan liberty. In 1866 the monastery sheltered numerous Cretans who were involved in the island's resistance against Turkish occupation. Overwhelmed by the Turkish besieging forces, the abbot is said to have decided to blow up the garrison rather than surrender, and gave the order to ignite the ammunition store, causing hundreds of casualties on both sides. The event is commemorated each year in November (see **Events**).
The monastery is situated in beautiful countryside in the hills to the south east of Rethymnon. During the process of restoration a variety of architectural styles from different periods has been revealed. There is a regular bus service from Rethymnon to the monastery which is open 0800-1900.

Moni Asomaton: See **RETHYMNON - EXCURSION.**

Moni Gonia: This 17thC Venetian monastery at Kolimbari, 23 km west of Chania, houses a collection of fine icons and precious objects. You can reach the monastery by car, or by bus from Kydomies St. in Chania (get off at Kastelli, then walk for 2 km). The building is closed daily between 1300 and 1530.

Moni Preveli: See **RETHYMNON - EXCURSION.**

Moni Toplou: An isolated monastery, resembling a fortress, which sits on a plateau surrounded by hills at the eastern end of Crete. It has traditionally been associated with the defence of Cretan liberty, and was also reputed to possess great wealth. A stone to the left of the entrance to the church is inscribed with a 2ndC BC treaty between Egypt and the Cretan towns of Itanos and Iierapytna (Ierapetra). Inside are some beautiful icons, the most important of which is *Lord Thou Art Great* by Ioannis Kornaros (1770). See **AGIOS NIKOLAOS - EXCURSION 1.**

Moni Vondrisi: See HERAKLION - EXCURSION 1.

Myths and Legends: Zeus, supreme ruler of the gods, was hidden in a cave on Crete at his birth to escape being killed by his father, Kronos, who was fearful of being overthrown. The Diktaean Cave (see AGIOS NIKOLAOS - EXCURSION 2, **A-Z**) and the Idaian Cave (see HERAKLION - EXCURSION 2, **A-Z**) are most associated with legends concerning Zeus, who went on to abduct the Princess Europa from Phoenicia and carry her to Crete where she bore three sons - one of whom was Minos, who eventually became king of the island and founded the Minoan dynasty which held sway over most of the Greek islands and many parts of the mainland. King Minos' wife Pasiphae, having fallen in love with a bull, gave birth to Asterius, commonly known as the Minotaur - the monster endowed with the head of a bull and the body of a man. The creature was condemned to be hidden from sight, imprisoned in the Labyrinth at Knossos, which Minos ordered to be constructed by Daedalus. The king then imposed a tribute on Athens, forcing the city to send seven maidens and seven boys, every seven years, to be fed to the Minotaur. This continued until Theseus arrived,

voluntarily, on the island as one of the fated fourteen. He fell in love with King Minos' daughter, Ariadne, who, on Daedalus' suggestion, gave him a sword and a ball of thread enabling him to kill the Minotaur and escape from the Labyrinth. Daedalus was banished to his own labyrinth for betraying King Minos and helping in the escape plot, and his son Icarus was forced to join him. Daedalus, always the ingenious inventor, then constructed wax and feather wings with which the two could effect their escape from the island. Before their flight the father warned his son from flying either to close to the sea, and wetting his feathers, or to near the sun, which would melt the wax. Forgetting his instructions Icarus flew too high and fell to his death in the sea now known as the Icarian Sea.

Newspapers: Foreign newspapers, both tabloids and the quality press, are widely available at kiosks the day after publication. The English-language *Athens News* is also found everywhere there is a market for it, and covers both Greek and international news.

Nightlife: Cretans tend to eat late and often stay up till the early hours drinking and dancing. Most discos and bars are intended to cater for the tourists so if you want a more authentic evening try a bouzouki bar. The NTOG offices (see **Tourist Information**) can provide up-to-date information on current theatre and dance performances, although the best examples of traditional folk dancing (see **A-Z**) are probably to be seen at the local saints' day celebrations known as *panegyria* (see **Festivities**). There are also cinemas in Crete, which are usually open-air and show foreign films subtitled into Greek. See NIGHTLIFE, RESTAURANTS, **Eating Out, Food**.

Nudism: Topless sunbathing is tolerated in Greece, but nudism is officially prohibited and can greatly offend local people. Despite this it can be practised with discretion on some of the remoter stretches of sand and in more isolated coves.

Opening Times: These vary considerably from place to place and season to season, are subject to frequent changes and can also depend on the vagaries of the owner or manager. This is especially true of the discos and nightclubs (see NIGHTLIFE) which exist purely to cater for tourists and will open earlier if there is a demand for them, or close when there are too few customers to make it worthwhile staying open. Greece does not run to a strict timetable! The following times, therefore, are very general:
NTOG offices (see **Tourist Information**) - 0800-1400, 1700-2000 Mon.-Fri., 0800-1400 Sat.- Sun. and in the low season.
Post offices (see **A-Z**) - 0800-1900 Mon.-Fri. in some resorts, 0800-1400 Mon.-Fri. in others.
Banks - 0800-1400 Mon. to Thurs., 0800-1330 Fri. In addition, during the summer, one bank in each of the provincial capitals re-opens between 1700-1900 and also opens on Sat. for changing money.
Restaurants - 1200-1500, 2000 till late (most stop serving at midnight).
Shops - 0800-1430 Mon., Wed., Sat.; 0800-1400, 1730-2000 Tues., Thurs., Fri. (some shops in most busy resorts now stay open in the afternoon to cater for the shopping habits of tourists).
OTE offices (see **Telephones and Telegrams**) - in Heraklion and Chania stay open 24 hr, but in the smaller towns they can close at 1500.

Orientation: Crete, the largest and most southerly of the Greek islands, is divided up into four nomes or provinces - Heraklion, Chania, Lasithi and Rethymnon, the capitals of which are Heraklion (also the capital of the island), Chania, Rethymnon and Agios Nikolaos. We have followed this geographic distinction in the arrangement of the 'topics' part of this book, which is divided into four alphabetical sections headed by the name of the provincial capital.
We strongly suggest that you purchase as detailed a road map of Crete as you can possibly find before you come to the island and begin exploring its less accessible regions, for although the main north-coast roads are well signposted and maintained, the secondary and dirt roads of the remoter inland and south-coast areas can still present difficulties (see **Driving**). The NTOG offices (see **Tourist Information**) in the provincial capitals or at the airports can provide you with town maps pinpointing the chief sights, hotels, *etc.*
In Greek addresses the street number follows the street name, but outside the city centre the number that appears in this position may represent a block rather than individual premises (the number of which may appear afterwards in brackets). In giving addresses we have tended to use the English for 'Street', 'Avenue' and 'Square', which, in Greek, are *Odhos, Leoforos* and *Platia* respectively.

Paleochora: See CHANIA - BEACHES.

Passports and Customs: A valid passport (or identity card for some EC visitors) is necessary, but no visa is required for stays of less than three months. If you want to stay longer apply for an extension from the local police (see **A-Z**) or the Aliens Bureau, Alexandras Av 173, Athens (tel: 6468103/7705711 ext. 379) - you may be asked to show proof of financial resources.
There is no limit on the amount of foreign cash you bring into Greece but to leave with a large sum you must either prove that you received it from outside the country during your stay or that you had it to begin with, so declare amounts over £350 on entry and keep exchange receipts to avoid problems. You are allowed to bring in 100,000 Drs in cash and take out up to 20,000 Drs.

Pets: Small domestic pets which have been vaccinated against rabies (see **A-Z**) within the last year and have a health.certificate are permitted into Greece.

Phaestos Palace: The second most important centre of Minoan civilization occupies a magnificent site only 5 km from the Libyan Sea, with views of the mountains and the Mesara Plain. The palace was first excavated by an Italian, Frederico Halbharr, at the beginning of this century. In contrast to Knossos, very little reconstruction work has been carried out. The ruins largely consist of the remains of a palace which was inhabited up to about 1450 BC. A second palace was built on the foundations of the original structure, and sections of its floor plan are still evident. The site comprises a central courtyard, state rooms, royal quarters, servants' quarters, storerooms and a theatre. Finds from the area, including pottery, jewellery and the undeciphered Phaestos Disk, are displayed in the Archeological Museum at Heraklion (see **HERAKLION - WHAT TO SEE**, **A-Z**). See **HERAKLION - EXCURSION 1**.

Police: Apart from the regular police, who wear green uniforms and deal with crime, traffic offences, *etc*, there is also the Tourist Police who wear a dark grey-blue uniform and wear badges (national flags) indicating which foreign languages they speak. Their role is to help tourists in trouble and investigate any complaints about hotels, restaurant prices, *etc*. There are police stations at Karaiskaki St., Chania (tel: 24477/22426); Vas. Georgiou St. 52, Rethymnon (tel: 28156/22333); Dikeossinis St., Heraklion (tel: 283190/282031); Omirou St. 7, Agios Nikolaos (tel.

22321/22251); and if you are in Sitia you can call 24200/22266. See **Crime and Theft**, **Emergency Numbers.**

Polyrrina: Ruins of a city, 49 km west of Chania, dating from the Roman and Byzantine eras. The Cyclopean walls can be traced back to the time of Homer and the aqueduct to the time of Hadrian. There are magnificent views down to the coast.

Post Offices: All registered letters and parcels should be handed over to the clerk unsealed as the contents will have to be checked. It is cheaper to buy stamps in post offices than at kiosks where they are 10% more expensive. *Poste restante* services are fairly reliable, but be sure to mark the name of the post office clearly. The main post offices are in Gianiri St. (near Eleftherias Sq), Heraklion; at Tzanakaki St. 3-5, Chania; at P. Koundouriotou St. 92, Rethymnon; at 28 Octovriou St., Agios Nikolao; in Kothri Sq, Ierapetra; and at Evrikes Antistasis St. 2, Sitia. Post boxes are yellow. See **Opening Times**.

Public Holidays: 1 Jan. (New Year's Day), 6 Jan. (Epiphany), 25 Mar. (Independence Day), First day of Lent (Clean Monday), Good Friday (moveable feast), Easter Monday (moveable feast), Ascension Day (moveable feast), 1 May (Labour Day), Whit Monday (moveable feast), 15 Aug. (Assumption), 28 Oct. (Ochi Day), 25 Dec. (Christmas Day), 26 Dec. (St Stephen's Day). See **Events**.

Rabies: There are no recorded cases of rabies on the island. See **Pets**.

Radio and TV: There are daily English-language news broadcasts and tourist information items on local radio and television in Crete. You should also be able to receive the BBC World Service and VOA (Voice of America) without much difficulty on a portable transistor radio, as well as the American Forces' station. Television programmes often include imported English and American series which are subtitled into Greek.

Religious Services: The only other services apart from those of the

Greek Orthodox Church are Roman Catholic Masses held at the Catholic churches in Heraklion, Chania, Rethymnon and Agios Nikolaos every Saturday and Sunday.

Rethymnon: The capital of the province of Rethymnon and the third-largest town on the island. Pop: 20,000.
Rethymnon is a pleasant place to visit, with its relatively slow pace of life, its beautiful sandy beach and its huge Venetian fortress (see **Rethymnon Fortezza**). The old town is particularly attractive and consists of a maze of tiny streets, a port which can only be used by small vessels, and aristocratic residences decorated by distinctive arches and fine stone stairways. Traditionally a cultural and intellectual centre, which hosts congresses, exhibitions and theatrical works, and houses several departments of the University of Crete, the town has produced leading academics, artists and writers, including, most recently, Pandelis Prevelakis whose *Tale of a Town* represents a powerful personal history of the town.
Rethymnon's liveliest area is around Petichaki Square, although the beach is also lined with restaurants and cafés. There is a wine festival in the municipal gardens every July (see **Events)** and in November there are festivites commemorating the 1866 explosion at the nearby Moni Arkadi (see **Events, A-Z**). See **RETHYMNON - BEACHES, EXCURSION, NIGHTLIFE, RESTAURANTS, WALK, WHAT TO SEE.**

Rethymnon Fortezza: This massive fort was built in the 16thC by the Venetians in order to protect the town from raiding pirates. Maps from that period show that the structure originally contained barracks, a military governor's residence, a hospital and arsenals. Despite its strategic position the fort fell to the Turks in the middle of the 17thC. The ramparts, however, are especially well preserved and offer good views over the town and coastline. The centre is dominated by the large domed mosque of Ibrahim Han. See **RETHYMNON - WALK, WHAT TO SEE.**

Rimondi Fountian: This early-17thC fountain, facing the bustling cafés around Petichaki Square in Rethymnon, was named after the Venetian rector Alvise Arimondi. It is richly decorated with columns

and lions' heads, and once served as an important source of drinking water for the town's inhabitants. See **RETHYMNON - WALK, WHAT TO SEE**.

Saint Titus: The patron saint of Crete and the first bishop of Gortys (see **A-Z**). St Titus was an early Christian missionary to the island, directed there by St Paul in his New Testament *Epistle to Titus*. The Basilica of Agios Titus in Gortys (see **HERAKLION - EXCURSION 1**) and the church of the same name at Heraklion (see **HERAKLION - WHAT TO SEE**) are named in memory of the saint.

Samaria Gorge: A walk through the famous gorge is one of the best-known excursions on Crete. The 18 km trek from the Omalos Plateau down to the south coast, or vice versa, is an extremely strenuous one, and can be tricky in places. Every year there are injuries and incidents (sometimes even heart attacks). You must, therefore, be reasonably fit and only attempt the walk with the proper clothing and footwear and protection from the sun. It is safest and most convenient to go with an organized tour as the guides carry radios with which to call for assistance. Many travel agencies sell tickets for the bus trip/walk (costs 2500-4000 Drs.). The gorge can only be entered between the months of May and October since the water level rises, making it impassable in winter. See **CHANIA - EXCURSION**.

Sendoni Cave: 45 km south east of Rethymnon on the outskirts of the village of Zoniana. The dimensions of this cave, which has only recently been opened to the public, are impressive - 500 m long and 3300 m^2. During the low season the key can be obtained from the keeper in the village (next to the church). See **Caves**.

Sfakia: A region, on the slopes of the White Mountains, which is renowned for defending Cretan liberty against foreign invasion and occupation. The capital, Chora Sfakion, was a flourishing commercial port up to the 18thC. Due to its geographical position, Sfakia remained quite independent from the rest of the island, and there are various monuments in the area which bear witness to its bloody and heroic past. The area is now subject to a tourist invasion due to the popularity of excursions to the Samaria Gorge (see **CHANIA - EXCURSION**, **A-Z**). Nevertheless, Sfakia manages to retain an air of fierce independence.

Shopping: See **Best Buys, Markets**.

Sitia: See **AGIOS NIKOLAOS - BEACHES, EXCURSION 1.**

Spili: See **RETHYMNON - EXCURSION**.

Spinalonga: A small island in the Bay of Mirabello which was, until 1957, a leper colony housing up to 400 patients. In earlier times the strategically important island was the site of a Venetian fortress designed to defend the coast against Turkish forces. Built in 1579, it managed to withstand various assaults before it was surrendered in 1715. You can still see its ruins, and those of the surrounding settlement.

Sport:
Fishing - rod fishing is permitted everywhere, but harpooning is limited to Falassarna, Sfinari, Sougia and Sfakia in the Chania region; Panormos and Agia Galini in the Rethymnon region; Agia Pelagia, Chersonisos, Malia, Lendas, Kaloi Limenes and Tsoutsouros in the Heraklion region; and Agios Nikolaos, Mohlos, Palekastro, Myrtos and around Spinalonga and Chryssi in the Lasithi district.
Tennis - Chania Tennis Club, Dimokratias St., tel: 0821-24010/21293; Heraklion Tennis Club, Dukos Beufaurt St., tel: 081-226152 (after 1400). Both have five courts and it is possible to arrange for lessons.
Horse riding - Karteros Riding Club, Amnisos, tel: 081-282005 (lessons and trekking).
Diving - Elounda Beach Hotel, Elounda, tel: 0841-41412; Peninsula Hotel, Agia Pelagia, tel: 081-289404.
Windsurfing - boards for hire at Neas Choras, Maleme, Halyves, Kournas Lake, Almyrida, Kastelli, Rethymnon, Agia Galini, Adele, Bali and Plakias, Chersonisos harbour, Malia, Agia Pelagia, Agios Nikolaos, Kalo Chorio, Elounda, Ierapetra and Sitia. See **Beaches**.
Water-skiing - instruction at Chania Marine Club, Akti Kanari, tel: 0821-24387; Chersonisos harbour; Malia; and Agia Pelagia.
Mountaineering and skiing - the Greek Alpine Club (EOS) has refuges at Volikas and Kallergi in the White Mountains, and on Mount Ida. For information and keys contact the EOS offices at Stratigou Tzanaki St. 90, Chania, tel: 0821-24647; Dikeosinis St. 53, Heraklion, tel: 081-287110; Arkadias St. 143, Rethymnon, tel: 0831-22411.

Taxis: Taxis are relatively cheap and plentiful, most villages have at least one taxi and there are lots in the resorts and provincial towns. Although most drivers are honest and friendly, make sure that the meter

ΑΡΟΣ
ΡΟΤΑΒΕΡΝΑ
FRISCHER FISCH
FRESH FISH
ISHSOUP
WORDFISH
trivsel
boutari

is running, and for longer journeys agree a price beforehand. There are the usual surcharges for items of luggage, journeys late at night, *etc*, plus a fee for waiting time. It may be worthwhile hiring a taxi for a day excursion when the bus times prove inconvenient, especially if there are enough of you to share the cost. See **Tipping, Transport**.

Telephones and Telegrams: Metered international phone calls can be made from OTE (Greek Telecommunications Organization) offices or from phone boxes distinguished by an orange band, which take 5, 10 and 20 Drs coins. The main OTE offices are at Tzanakaki St. 3-5, Chania; Koundourioti St., Rethymnon; Minotavrou St. (behind Venizelos Sq), Heraklion; 25 Martiou St., Agios Nikolaos; Koraka St., Ierapetra; and Sifis St., Sitia. You may find that you have to queue for rather a long time, and the waiting time for connections can also be considerable.

To direct dial abroad dial 00 followed by the code for the country (UK - 44, USA - 1, Ireland - 353), then remember to omit the first 0 of the city code.

International Operator	161.
Local Operator	151.
Directory Enquiries	131.
Telegrams (in Greece)	155.
International Telegrams	165.
Telexes	181.

See **Emergency Numbers**.

It is cheaper to phone abroad between 2100-0900 and at weekends. Telegrams can be sent from OTE offices or by phone (see above). See **Opening Times**.

Time Difference: Two hours ahead of GMT.

Tipping: A service charge is included in hotel and restaurant bills, but it is also customary to leave a tip if you are satisfied with the service provided. Taxi drivers and hairdressers expect a 10% tip and waiters about 5%. You should give hotel porters 50 Drs per bag and leave your chambermaid 100 Drs when you leave.

Toilets: Public toilets are usually situated in public parks and in town squares - and they are often filthy! Those in bus stations, tavernas and bars may be a bit better, but still tend to be of an unpleasantly low standard of hygiene. Remember not to flush used toilet paper down the toilet as it will block up the narrow waste pipes characteristic of Greek plumbing. There is always a bin provided for their disposal. It is a wise precaution to carry tissues or toilet paper with you.

Tourist Information: The National Tourist Organization of Greece (NTOG), also known as the EOT (Ellinikos Organismos Tourismou), have offices manned by helpful, multilingual staff who will provide you with information on excursions, accommodation, ferry times, *etc*, as well as useful brochures, maps and timetables. These are at Akti Tombazi 6, Chania, tel: 26426 (see **CHANIA - WHAT TO SEE**); Xanthoudidou St., Eleftherias Sq, Heraklion, tel: 222487; on the seafront at Rethymnon, tel: 29148; and at the airports (see **A-Z**). See **Opening Times**.

Transport: Buses are the most common way of getting around the island, although their timetables can sometimes be restrictive and can also change frequently. Hiring a car allows you much more flexibility if you want to explore the island, but petrol is expensive. Taxis, especially if you can get together with others to share the cost, are another good alternative both for excursions and for getting from A to B. Hiring a motorbike or moped can give you greater freedom of movement, but be warned - every year there are a large number of accidents due to the poor condition of the roads, lack of experience and carelessness. Quite often it is possible, and fun, to hire local fishing boats to take you to remote beaches and small offshore islands where you can snorkel and sunbathe away from the crowds. See **Accidents and Breakdowns, Bicycle and Motorbike Hire, Buses, Car Hire, Driving, Ferries, Taxis, Yachts**.

Traveller's Cheques: See **Money**.

Vathipetro: The recently-discovered site of a large Minoan villa set

F-3
YT
38

in the middle of a fertile agricultural area 15 km south of Heraklion. The original multistorey building contained large rooms and basement workshops. Many interesting objects have been found here relating to the everyday life of the time, including wine and oil presses, weaving tools and what was probably a kiln. The site is presently open only on Mondays and Fridays (0800-1530).

Venizelos, Eleftherios (1864-1936): One of Greece's leading political figures. Born in Mournies (near Chania) in 1864, he attempted to lead a revolution in 1905. The revolt failed, but Venizelos eventually became Prime Minister of Greece in 1910. He was the architect of the Union of Crete with Greece in 1913 and is a greatly revered historical figure on Crete where there are various memorials to him (you can see his statue in Platia Eleftherias - Liberty Square - in Heraklion). There are also exhibits relating to him in Chania's Historical Museum and Archives (see CHANIA - WHAT TO SEE) and Venizelos House. He died in exile in Paris in 1936, having survived two assassination attempts, and is buried in Akrotiri (see CHANIA - BEACHES).

Yachts: Any yacht entering Greek waters is obliged to put into a designated entry point where the yacht's transit log must be handed over to the authorities. In the case of Crete, these are at the provincial capitals which all have marinas. The harbours of Chania, Soudha, Kastelli Kissamou, Paleochora, Rethymnon, Panormas, Agia Galini, Heraklion, Chersonisos, Agios Nikolaos, Sitia and Ierapetra can all provide fresh water, fuel and electricity. Chania also has a yacht-repair service and there is a small repair yard at Agios Nikolaos. Contact the following for further information:
Chania Marine Club (NOX), Akti Kanari, tel: 0821-24387; Rethymnon Marine Club (NOP), in Agios Nikolaos, tel: 0831-29881; Agios Nikolaos Marine Club (NAOAN), tel: 0841-22832; Heraklion 'Café Marina' (NOH), Venetian harbour, tel: 081-221128.
It is possible to hire yachts with crews, but this is extremely expensive.

Youth Hostels: There are youth hostels in the most popular north coast resorts such as Agios Nikolaos, Chania, *etc*, but the number changes from year to year so check with the local NTOG office (see **Tourist Information**) to find out if there is one where you want to go. The facilities offered in these are generally very basic and stays are often limited to five days, but conditions are clean, you can often cook your own food and, above all, they are very cheap. Theoretically you will need an International Youth Hostel Association membership card which can be obtained at the Greek headquarters at Dragatsanion St. 4, Athens (if you did not acquire one before you left home). However, the chances are that you will not be asked to produce this. See **Accommodation**, **Camping**.

Zakros Palace: Nikolaos Platon identified this site at the eastern end of Crete, 47 km from Sitia, as the fourth-largest centre of the Minoan civilization after earlier excavations (at the beginning of the century) of the ancient town had been abandoned by the British archeologist, David G. Hogarth. Full-scale excavation began again in 1962 and the palace was found very quickly. It was largely destroyed in 1450 BC when its inhabitants fled with their belongings. Nevertheless the site has yielded a great many interesting archeological finds and treasures, some of which can be seen in Sitia Museum and others in the Archeological Museum at Heraklion (see **HERAKLION - WHAT TO SEE, A-Z**). See **AGIOS NIKOLAOS - WHAT TO SEE**.